Grass, a There Were Trees

by
Krisha Stanworth

Strategic Book Publishing and Rights Co.

Strategic Book Publishing and Rights Co.
12620 FM 1960, Suite A4-507
Houston TX 77065
www.sbpra.com

ISBN: 978-1-62212-246-2

Dedicated to all parents apart.

I feel your pain.

Contents

Contents

PROLOGUE

I was born to parents from different nationalities and religions, and I was the last child in the family. Having been exposed to village life and its mentality, I soon formed a strong mind, but the village mentality forced feelings of rejection upon me.

I grew up among some family members who had been involved with the courts, which led to our rejection from some of the community members. This had also been experienced by other members of my immediate family.

I had ambitions, and they were not in the village where I had been brought up. Away from the village I was living a comfortable life. I had started travelling the world and had everything to look forward to.

On April 15, 1989 I was working as a barmaid in a local pub. It was a day that the world would never forget—the day of the Hillsborough Disaster, where 96 innocent Liverpool fans had been killed during an FA cup match.

Word spread like wildfire throughout the country, and it was only a matter of time before it reached the local pub where I was working.

Liverpool fans filtered through the doors of the pub, and their bewilderment was heart wrenching. We replaced beer with free tea and coffee and offered free access to the phone for all supporters to call home and loved ones.

That same day a man named Fred walked into the pub, and it changed the course of my life forever. I regret what ensued, and I am still dealing with the injuries I received to this day.

This book catalogues my journey through a traumatic period in my adult life in which I experienced domestic abuse, official corruption, and finding spirituality and a new way of dealing with and understanding my experiences.

INTRODUCTION

The book reflects a roller-coaster lifestyle that lasted 6 years. It is a true account of my journey of being a mum caring for my family to a woman investigated for serious crime. The judicial system forced life-changing decisions upon me and I consented to nothing. I'll explain the danger of association with family members with criminal records and how the judicial system used that association in a bid to secure conviction and control of my children. This book shows how the police initiated the coming together of a group of criminals, which ended in tragedy.

I had everything but was catapulted from a normal life into another life of total chaos and destruction, and this all happened without my consent. This lifestyle led, in my opinion, to the death of an innocent woman who had given most of her life to children torn from their parents. This woman provided these children with a purpose for family life, but hers was taken by one of the most evil people I have ever had the unfortunate experience of meeting.

The book reflects how you can never know the people you live with or your own children. Without realising it, I allowed a man to take control of both my children and me, and he was hell bent on ensuring I felt pain to gratify himself.

The family courts were asked to make a decision as to where my two children should reside.

It shows how someone who has personal issues can destroy, manipulate, and demonstrate mental health problems, while enforcing these illnesses onto innocent people to gain gratification for themselves. This demonstration was never taken into account or discovered when making legal decisions that would change the course of four people's lives forever.

The shock of everything concerned prevented me from speaking out, and as a result I was sentenced to a life of mental torture until one day things took an unexpected turn.

Names have been changed to hide the identity of the people involved, but this does not render the book false in anyway. The information contained within is true to the best of my knowledge, and this story documents a true life journey. This is how I learned to face my conscience to satisfy my purpose and to learn to grow spiritually. I would like you to understand that some of the incidents overlap others and may seem out of sync, but incidents did overlap.

Chapter One
Aggravated Burglary

"Give me the keys for your car. I need to go somewhere."

"No, not till I see your driving license. We have had this conversation so many times, so why do you insist? Until you produce that there is no way you're taking my car."

The conversation follows this line for a few more minutes.

"OK, then will you at least take me where I need to go? It will only take you five minutes."

"Why can't you walk then?"

I found myself driving my then partner Fred and a young adolescence lad I had seen before to where Fred wanted dropping off.

"Funny place to be wanting dropped off at. It's a derelict pit yard by the looks of things. What you doing down here then?"

"Oh, nothing. Will you wait here because we will only be five minutes?"

"Do I have to? I've got the tea on and I know your five minutes."

But there I was sat waiting in a derelict pit yard.

"Come on. Hurry up," I kept saying to myself. I wanted to get back to do the tea and spend some time with my son who hadn't been in from school long before I had come out of the house. I was looking in the direction that Fred and the young adolescence lad had disappeared. Moments later the young adolescence lad came from a gap some way down the yard, and he was running. He opened the door at the back of the car, got in, and immediately hit the floor crying.

"I want my mum! I want my mum!"

"What's up, love? What are you crying for? What's happened?" I asked in a concerned voice.

No reply came from the lad other than him repeating he wanted his mother.

The driver's side door flung open and before I knew it I had been hit in the face and dragged out of my seat, facing Fred's angry face.

"You have five seconds to get in the passenger seat," ordered Fred. The look on his face spelled trouble.

I was stunned, shocked, and in pain. I wanted to ask, "Why have you hit me in the face? What had happened? What was all this about?" but before I knew it Fred was forcing me around the bonnet and to the passenger door.

"Move or be left," Fred barked at me.

I got in and we sped off. Fred was driving, and he placed a gun on the dashboard.

"What the …?" I tried to get out of my mouth, but my throat was tight. I couldn't believe I was sat staring at a gun.

"Shut up or you will be next! You, boy, shut up your snivelling or else! You wanted to come to the big leagues. Well now you're here so shut up!"

The lad kept whispering repeatedly in a crying moan that he wanted his mother.

The journey home took minutes. Our car pulled up on the drive beside the house. Blood was streaming from my nose, all over my clothes and the car. Stunned and in shock, I didn't know what to do.

"Stay there!" Fred barked. He was walking in the direction of the house and came back within seconds. He approached the back door to the car where the young lad laid almost on the floor, still crying.

"Out, now! I'll show you! Get in the house."

Fred turned to me.

"And you move it!" he growled.

The tone of Fred's voice made me realise he meant business. Minutes later, we were in the kitchen of the house.

"Shut up, sniffling boy! You wanted this so don't be crying now! Welcome to the big world of crime."

"What? What have you done?" I asked in between trying to wipe the blood from my face and trying to understand why I had been attacked in the manner I had. Why was this lad crying? In fact, he was petrified.

Fred said, "Tell her! Tell her what we have done! Tell her how you wanted to get into the big league of crime! How I told you once in that league there would be no turning back, and look at you now—you're a snivelling idiot!"

The lad never spoke, just sobbed.

Fred demanded, "Or shall I tell her?"

Fred turned to me.

"We, all three of us, have just committed our first serious crime together. So if either of you think I'm going down for this on my own, forget it. There is no escaping me now, and if we get caught we will all be doing big time."

The boy sobbed harder.

"What you on about crime? What crime? What have you done? Why is this lad in such a state? Tell me what you have done! Crime? Crime? I've committed no crime! What are you talking about? Why have you got a gun? And why have you punched me in the face? Tell me!" I shouted at Fred.

I stood staring Fred right in the face. I was furious and couldn't believe what Fred had just said. He was wearing a broad smile and had a smug look upon his face. His chin tightened as he spoke.

"You think that you can ever leave me now? You will never be rid of me! I've made sure of that. You see, I and Boyo have just committed aggravated burglary and you, my dear, were the driver of the car that we travelled in. You are an accomplice in this crime." Fred enjoyed saying the words. He loved the control.

He stood waving the handgun in front of the boy. He was instilling fear, and he knew he would get his desired effect.

"Don't tell me you shot someone." I said. My chest was tightening. *Please God no! Please don't let someone have died.*

The boy sobbed harder. The sound went right through me, and I turned to look at him. This didn't seem real. In an instant Fred was almost on top of the boy, who sat with his head down on the table. Fred thrust the gun toward the boy's head.

"No! Don't shoot him!" I begged.

I could hardly breathe, and in a panic I stepped toward them both.

"Stay where you are or I swear I will hurt him," Fred grimaced through his teeth.

He's lost it. What the bloody hell? I knew I had better stay still. Lord knows what he was going to do next. "Please don't kill him!" I prayed to God.

Suddenly Fred turned away from the boy and went upstairs. I found that I couldn't move—I was rooted to the spot. The boy sat there, head down and still sobbing. I ran through my mind the episodes of the last ten minutes or so.

This is a bloody nightmare. What the bloody hell had happened? Robbery! Guns! What the fuck? Had I missed something?

I heard footsteps coming down the stairs. I heard voices. I could hear Fred's, the lodger Barry and my young son, Roy. My heart started racing.

Oh my God! My son, Roy!. He is near my son, Roy! Please God don't let him get hurt.

I started moving toward the living room, making my way to my son.

I heard the front door open and then close. I realised that my son was now out of the house.

Making my way toward the front door I was met with Fred in the doorway to the kitchen.

"Fucking tell me, you bastard, what have you done? Where is my son? Who the fuck are you? Who do you think you are?" I asked in an angry voice.

"I'll tell you who I am. I'm the man that will control everything you say and do from now on." Fred loved the control. I could see it in his face.

"Like fuck! No one controls me. I've done nothing wrong. I'm going to call the police. You're a nut case!" I said, walking toward the phone that hung in the kitchen.

In an instant Fred was at the boy's head with the gun against it. Fred was staring straight at me.

"No you won't. You will do as you're told, won't you?"

Looking me straight in the eye, Fred spoke in a cold controlled voice. I knew he meant business.

"He put the gun to the woman in the bedroom," the boy chirped up suddenly.

"That's right! I did, and if I ever had to use it, don't think I wouldn't," Fred snarled in response.

"You've done what? What woman? You are dangerous. Take that gun away from his head now!" I demanded, full of fear and dread.

Seconds hung in the air like hours, and all senses were heightened. The room felt full of electricity, and I had no idea what was going to happen. Nothing could be taken for granted with Fred. Only an hour earlier I would never have believed myself or anyone would be in the situation I was now faced with.

Fred suddenly walked away from the lad.

"Yes, that's right—we have just robbed a businessman's home and his wife was there. We have taken what she says are the only wages and wage slips in the house, and I had to force it out of her. We know that there is more, but this crazy little bastard ran out of the house so I never got the time to find out where the rest was," Fred spurted out.

"You can't do something like that to someone. Wages? What wages? Who's the businessman? Do you realise what you have done? I asked.

"No, what *we* have done," said Fred, pointing at all three of us in turn with the gun.

"I've done nothing but give you a lift. I'm phoning the police!" I said, moving in the direction of the phone.

Fred lunged for the wires attached to the phone and yanked them from the socket.

"You will be phoning no one if you know what's good for you! Do you want to keep your son? Do you want him visiting you in prison for years to come? You ever try that again and I will make sure that your son hates you and never wants to see you again." Fred said in a cold blunt voice, almost robotic.

"Bollocks, I've done nothing. You are crazy and dangerous. You need locking away, not me. My son won't be going to any prison to visit me because I've done nothing wrong." I shouted my words at him.

Fred spun round toward the boy, ordering him to his feet and pulling him out of the door. Fred followed close behind, giving him orders to get in the car. Then Fred turned around and said to me, "Don't even think about it. You remember what I've told you and don't think for one minute I'm kidding or I won't drop you in it."

He was like a man possessed; pure evil poured from him. No sooner had Fred and the boy left, our lodger Barry and my son Roy walked in the back door.

Chapter Two
The Business

Within a few months after the Robbery, Fred had decided that we would have a business. I said immediately that I wanted nothing to do with any business venture. I was told I had no say in the matter and this was something that needed to be done as soon as possible.

"No! No! No! There is no way I'm committing myself to any business. I wouldn't have a clue where to start," I protested.

"You don't have a say in the matter," snarled Fred.

He was angry and I could tell.

"You can't make me do something like that if I don't want to," I snarled back.

"I've made an appointment with someone who will explain everything we need to know about running our own business. They will show us how to put together a business plan so we can approach the bank, so get used to the idea." Fred meant every word he said.

***

Within the week we were both sat in front of a business adviser and all the necessary information was handed to us in the form of charts, leaflets, and contact numbers. We left with the adviser saying, "Don't hesitate to contact me if you have any further questions." As we left his office, Fred instructed me that I was going home because he had somewhere to go; I had no say in the matter. I feared this man's behaviour, and I knew first-hand he just did what he wanted and he was unpredictable.

***

The following week Fred announced that an appointment had been made with the bank manager and we both had to attend to secure a business loan.

"I'm not going to a meeting to see a bank manager because I'm not having my own business!" I snapped at Fred.

I was sick of telling him that I wasn't interested, and now he was telling me that an appointment had been made. No, I was going to stand my ground—I wasn't going!

The date of the appointment for the bank came around and all morning I was arguing with Fred. I was adamant that I wasn't going. If I had wanted a business I would start one myself and certainly not with Fred. I told him this. In a flash Fred had picked up a kitchen knife and he had me on the floor with the knife to my throat.

"When I say you will do something," Fred hissed through his teeth at me, "you are going to do it! You are not going to disobey—you will just do as I say."

"Like fuck! You are a crazy man and anyone in their right mind wouldn't open business with you!" I shouted.

The next thing I knew Fred had his hands around my throat. After a second he let go, saying he could easily end my life if he wanted to. Fred left the house for the meeting at the bank, and I stayed home. He could do whatever he wanted, but I was signing nothing legal with him.

He was back a couple of hours later all full of himself, saying that we had been approved by the bank for a business loan and that the money would be in a new business account within a few days. Fred said the bank manager had accepted that I was feeling ill on that day and he would catch up with me at a later date to sign the papers. I again told Fred I wouldn't sign any legal papers and I wasn't having any business. Fred just stared hard at me, but I wasn't going to change my mind.

Early evening, after I had settled my son Roy to sleep, I went downstairs to watch television. Fred was sat in the living room and there was no mistaking that he was not happy. He made me feel that I should not be in my home, and the tension was unbearable in the room. That was it; I snapped. I told Fred he would have to leave my home because I couldn't stand the things he did, he was unpredictable, and his presence was making me feel uncomfortable.

Fred flew into a violent rage and before I knew it he was beating me up. He hit me several times about the upper part of my head. He was hissing all the evil things he was going to do to me if I so much as thought about ever leaving him. I tried to ask him to stop hitting me, but I just wasn't getting through to him. He was a man possessed, and he had so much hatred in him. After he stopped his assault on me and I was sat in the armchair daring not to make a sound, I heard my young son Roy upstairs stirring in his sleep. Fred immediately was on his feet; he turned to me, instructing that I stay where I was and he would see to my son.

While Fred was upstairs I wept silently. Then I had the idea it would be best to just end my life. I felt that I would never escape this man and I was fearful of him. I went to the medicine cabinet in the kitchen and took a handful of Paracetamol and any other tablets that I could get my hands on. I then went and sat back down in the room.

***

I half woke up and tried opening my eyes. I could hear wheels moving on a floor and bright lights. A man stood above me; I couldn't understand what he was saying. I felt sick.

I woke again and this time I was in a bed in what appeared to be a hospital ward.

"Hello," A doctor introduced himself to me.

"That was a close call. You certainly gave us a scare. The nurse will take some blood and then I will see you later," he said.

The doctor went and the nurse took my blood. About fifteen minutes later the nurse came back and asked me to follow her as I was going to see the doctor. In the doctor's room he explained that my attempt at suicide was not a cry for help. And he knew I had meant to kill myself. I just stayed mute. The doctor continued, saying that my "common-law husband" would be here soon because he had requested he attend the meeting with him.

"Common-law husband? I don't think so!" I said, "I'm still married but separated from my husband, and I don't want Fred anywhere near me. I don't want to ever see him again and I want my son away from him now!"

"Now calm down. We will get this sorted out when your partner gets here," said the doctor

He wasn't listening. Before I knew it there came a knock on the door and a nurse walked in, followed by Fred. I put my head down. The doctor spoke with Fred, asking him what problems, if any, were there? Was I depressed? Fred responded that as far as he knew nothing was wrong. I was fuming inside. How dare they speak to this mad man and ask him questions about me? There was no point saying anything; they obviously thought I was nuts or something. I was discharged from hospital with no follow-up appointment and into the care of Fred. Worst of all, I had no say in any decision made about me. I felt that I was not worth listening to.

***

A week passed and Fred returned from a morning out somewhere. "I've found us some premises and I have paid three months' rent up front. I will take you to see them later today, but I have to go and sort out some shelving and things for the shop premises first." Fred spoke with such pride.

***

Within a couple of weeks Fred had the shop up and running. I still hadn't seen a bank manager or signed any paper to link me to this business venture, and I had no intention to. One lunch time I returned to the shop to find Fred there with the bank manager. Immediately the bank manager brought up the signing of the papers and how I needed to sign them. I said I didn't have the time at that moment because I couldn't think of anything else to say.

"Oh, don't worry. She will be free about two this afternoon. Could we come to the bank and see you then?" Fred asked. So it was set—the appointment for me to sign some business papers. How was I going to get out of this situation?

At the bank a few hours later and after I received threats from Fred, we were asked to go into an office and there on the table was a file of papers, which I automatically thought, "Business contract." The bank manager said that I would have to sign my home as security against the business loan.

I immediately said, "No! That's something I'm not prepared to do. The house is not just mine and it is still under a mortgage, so I'm not signing under those conditions. Sorry!"

I could tell Fred was furious, and the bank manager looked on dumbfounded, but there was no way I was signing my house over. Fred had control of everything, but the house was also my husband's. He would have needed to sign to agree and that definitely wasn't going to happen, no matter how much I was beaten and threatened by Fred. The bank manager realised there was no way I was going to sign those papers, so he said we would both have to sign another contract that wasn't secured. He asked if we could wait while he got a different contract ready so that it could be signed that day.

Fred immediately spoke. "Yes we will wait."

I glared at him and him at me. The tension was electrifying. The bank manager returned a short while later with the new contract. This time the business loan had both our signatures on it. I really didn't want any part of this and I felt so ill. The bank manager was saying something that really didn't register, and as I glanced up he was looking for something in a cabinet behind him. He had his back turned to where I and Fred sat. Suddenly Fred moved forward in his chair and took some papers from the top of a pile in the open file. I just looked and thought, "What are you doing?" but before I could say anything Fred had the papers inside his jacket and the

19

bank manager had turned around to face us, still talking away. I sat frozen to the chair. What had Fred done, and why? Dread filled my entire body.

***

A few months into the business, the bank manager appeared in the shop's doorway.

"Hi, is Fred in?" he asked.

"No, sorry". He won't be here till about three this afternoon. Is there anything I can help with?" I asked.

"I'd prefer to speak to Fred. Could you ask him to contact me? It is quiet urgent," said the bank manager.

"Well, can I help?" I asked again. I could tell the bank manager didn't want to speak to me, but if it concerned the business I wanted to know.

"I want to speak to him about the takings from the shop," the bank manager said.

"What about the takings?"

"Well, as I say, I'd prefer to talk to Fred, but I would like to know why there has been no takings deposited with the bank for more than a week," he explained.

"But takings have been put in the night safe. I should know—I am with him when he puts them in," I replied.

"The night safe is checked every morning and there have been no takings from this business. There have been empty cloth bank bags and a filled-in slip from this business but no money inside the bag. That's why I said I needed to speak with Fred," explained the bank manager.

The bank manager left the shop, and I was left fuming. I just knew what the bank manager had to say was the truth, but I still hoped it wasn't. I had been there when Fred had put the money bag in the night safe containing the takings from our business, but somehow that had gone missing when the night safe had been checked the following day.

When Fred returned I explained what had been said by the bank manager. He insisted that I go with him immediately to the bank to sort out this situation. At the bank Fred explained to the bank manager that he had indeed deposited the takings from the business and if the bag containing our monies was empty when the bank checked the bag then someone at the bank was taking the money. As soon as Fred said that, a voice in my head said, "He's done it!" I don't know how he had done it, but it would only be him that would somehow work out a way to get his hands on the business's takings and be able to blame the bank.

Fred was insisting that the bank bring the police because there must be someone corrupt working at the bank, but they had targeted the wrong business and he wasn't standing for it. For some reason the bank manager didn't bring the police and said in future all takings must be banked in person.

That's all that I was aware that happened in relation to the missing takings. It was bit strange really because I would have expected the police to have been brought immediately by the bank.

***

A few weeks later, Fred woke me up with a start.

"Come on—get up! We have a very busy day ahead of us and we already have queues forming," Fred said.

"What? What you on about? The business is closed today," I replied.

"Yes the shop is, but the garden sale isn't," Fred said.

"Garden sale? What garden sale?" I asked, still trying to come around from sleep.

"The one in our garden! So come on—get up now!" Fred disappeared through the bedroom door.

What was he on about? Garden sale? We were not having a garden sale. I got up, washed and dressed, and went downstairs. There on the garden was the entire content of our business and loads of people looking and buying the stock. Fred had a till set up, and the young lad Barry who lived with us was working the cash register.

I asked Fred, "What is going on?"

"I will tell you later."

I went on to say that I wanted to know now, but Fred gave me that threatening stare and I had learned not to question further if I didn't want a beating. After the garden sale had finished, he told me that he was closing our business. I had not been consulted about anything—he made all the decisions. I was told by Fred that he had sold all the fixture and fittings also, and he informed me that he was going to put all the money that he had received for the stock and the fixture and fittings into the bank the following morning.

***

Early one morning a few days later, I was awoken by a loud knock on the house door. I sat up in bed and thought someone was in a rush to get my attention by the way they were pounding on the door.

"Don't answer that door!" Fred stated.

"I am—something is wrong. Someone wants me," I replied, getting out of bed and making my way downstairs.

The police stood there when I opened the door. They placed me under

21

arrest immediately. Before I knew it they were inside my home, and Fred also had been placed under arrest. My mother had stayed at my home the night before so she looked after my son Roy while the police took me to the police station for questioning.

In the custody suite at the police station Fred and the officer started arguing. Neither of us had been booked in at that stage, and a brawl between Fred and the officers broke out. As a result of that I was hit in the stomach by a police officer by accident. I wasn't fighting with anyone—it was all Fred.

The interview started some time later and I was informed I had been arrested on offenses of fraud and deception amounting to thousands of pounds in money, all revolving around the business I was a partner in. I sat mute. I couldn't believe what the police were doing to me, but life experience had taught me that if someone wants you to be responsible for something and they had an official capacity, then you stood no chance in clearing your name or innocence. I was later released on bail and charged with various offences. My legal representative who had been present throughout the interviews took me immediately to a nearby hospital because I wasn't feeling too well. I discovered at the hospital that I was about thirteen weeks pregnant and that the baby was dying inside me—probably because I had been hit in the stomach.

***

More than a year later Fred and I attended Crown Court to face the charges. We had entered a plea of not guilty, so we had to face a jury. The jury were sworn in and the trial began. During the first morning of the trial the judge had asked the prosecution to present him with what he called "Some missing paperwork, i.e., where was the business contract?" It appeared that the prosecution had misplaced it and then subsequently asked for an hour adjournment so they could get the document to court. The judge agreed to let the case be adjourned for an hour and released Fred and me on bail for that period. The jury was released also. One hour later we were all back in the courtroom, but still the prosecution could not produce the paperwork. The judge gave them a further two hours to produce the necessary papers so that the trial could continue. Once that time had elapsed we were yet again back in the courtroom and again the prosecution could not produce the paperwork. The judge subsequently ordered that the jury find both Fred and me not guilty of the charges brought before the courts. Once we were outside and all charges had been dismissed, Fred proceeded to tell me he knew nothing would happen because he had taken the contract on the day we had signed it in the bank.

Chapter Three
Highway Robbery

"Come on, love, you haven't been out for ages. Let's go for a run around in the car," said Fred.

"No, it's OK. I'm fine just staying in," I replied.

"I won't take no for an answer. Get ready, you're driving," Fred ordered.

My chest tightened and immediately I was back in that pit yard.

"No, I'm not going!" I said, trying to make my stand.

"Yes, you are." Moving closer to me Fred put himself right in my face. Later, I was driving.

Fred said, "We are going to see someone, and before you ask, it's a surprise."

I wasn't happy at all, and after trying to say no and demand that I saw no one, Fred didn't leave me any choice.

"I've told you before you do as I say—not as you want. Now you will drive me to where I want to go," he ordered.

I found I was driving toward a village I knew, and in an instant it hit me —this was where I'd recognised the young adolescence boy from.

"Oh no, I'm not going. I'm turning this car around and I'm going home!" I had a dread in my entire body. Moments later Fred ordered me to stop the car and we sat there in silence. I could have thrown up. The intense feeling was too much. The back door suddenly opened. I stared in the mirror and my worst fear was sat there, the young adolescence boy.

Then we were back on country roads. Fred ordered, "Stop the car! Right here will do fine."

They left me in the car alone, and panic and dread took over. I felt so ill. What were they up to? I knew that they must have been up to no good.

What were they doing? Oh God please don't let this be happening to me again. Please! I just want to die. I have never done anything in my life to warrant this." I was thinking this while my entire body felt exhausted.

Voices came from the direction of the road they had just gone down. I looked in the mirror. There they were, laughing out loud, and they seemed to be throwing something into the hedge at the side of the road.

They both got in the car and a conversation struck up between them.

"That was great! Weren't it? So now you have a liking for the big time? Easy, isn't it? Did you see their faces? A picture, weren't it?" Fred was so proud of whatever he had just achieved.

The conversation unfolded between them and what came out was just too much for me to bear. I drove, thinking, "How could anyone do such a thing?"

I stopped the car at a set of traffic lights and jumped out. I just needed to get away. I couldn't stand what they were saying, and they thought it was a good thing. I knew things were getting more serious and they didn't care who they hurt. I just daren't go to the police. I wouldn't know where or how to start explaining how I knew these things.

Where was I going? I had no idea. I just couldn't sit there anymore listening to what they described as their latest victory. They spoke about it with such pride. I'd listened to how they had walked back down the lane where I'd been parked and in broad daylight approached a car where two people sat. At gunpoint they had ordered them to strip, hand over their money and bank cards, and give them their pin numbers and addresses. The couple had been ordered to not get out of their car for ten minutes after they had left. They were bragging how they had thrown all the victims' clothes in the hedge and were assuming that both people were married to other people and having an affair. They thought it highly amusing when the couple would have to admit to their partners what had happened and why they had been down the lane in the first place. That's *if* they reported the incident. They felt sure it wouldn't get reported. Fred and his partner said, "They are married and they wouldn't dare."

***

Within a week Fred and the adolescence boy had robbed and victimised others on the same stretch of road. They would sit and talk how they were blackmailing a woman from the Manchester region, how she was just handing them money so they would not tell her husband.

They showed no mercy for their victims, and their talk suggested more acts of crime. It was not long before it was every day the two were fully active criminals.

More people were introduced into their circle of criminal activity, and not one of them thought that what they were doing to these innocent people or their families was wrong. Fred was demonstrating that he had no consideration for his home life or that of my son. It was clear that he would not change his way of life and I just prayed that the police would soon put everything together and he would be arrested and I could move away to somewhere he would never find me again. Then my son and I could start a new life and I could learn to live again.

Chapter Four
Meeting Who?

In December 1991 I gave birth to my second son Reggie. In January 1992, we were all at home relaxing.

"Some of my friends have come to see you and the baby," said Fred.

Seconds later two men stood there.

"Hi, I'm Silver," said the first man.

"I'm Blondie. Let's have a look at the little one then," said the second man.

Blondie handed me some flowers and a card. I seemed to recognise their faces; I remembered I had seen them before. They were two of Fred's mates who had parked outside the house several times before. A few minutes later Fred and his two mates sat talking, and I switched my ears off to the majority of their conversation. I'd heard some bits of their conversation but just couldn't be bothered to listen. Who is he? What was the word on the street? Someone must know him? They were saying these sorts of things to each other.

"The only reason he got away was because of the fog and the fact he'd used the Pennine Trail and no one expected that route to be used," one of the friends said.

The conversation was about an estate agent who had been kidnapped. I thought that was a weird thing to be talking about. Once the friends had left I asked Fred if there had been anything more happened with regards to this estate agent being kidnapped while I had been in hospital.

"No! Why?" Fred asked.

I went on to say I was only asking because I'd heard some of the conversation between him and his friends.

***

Christmas was approaching. The mood was being set in the house for the holiday and my eldest son Roy was getting excited at the thought that

Father Christmas was coming soon. We had a new baby in the house, and everything was ready for the main day. Christmas came and went and had been quiet enjoyable for my son and me. I had always loved Christmas and was glad my eldest son enjoyed this time of year too. In January 1992, we were all at home relaxing.

It was late one evening. I was lying on the sofa with the new-born baby; my eldest son Roy sat using his computer at the back of the room behind the sofa. Fred was in the kitchen. Suddenly and without warning Fred shot past the sofa that I was laying on, his arm stretched out behind him, his hand clutching my eldest son's arm, demanding that I got up and came upstairs. "Quick. Hurry," he barked.

"Why? What's up?" I replied. *What's his problem?*

I looked toward the window and there stood a man looking in. Most of his body was just a silhouette. He had something in his hands, and he was pointing a gun at me. My heart almost burst in my chest with fear, and before I knew it I was heading off upstairs. It must have been automatic pilot. I could hear feet running down the drive at the side of the house and Fred shouting, "Help! Help! Someone get the police—they have a gun."

I heard someone reply to those cries for help, "We are phoning the police."

I was certain his shouts were coming from the bathroom, so I tried the door. Locked!

"Open this door now! What the hell is happening?" I asked, holding the baby close to me.

"Quick—get inside." Fred put out his hand through the door and dragged me into the bathroom.

"What the hell is happening? Who's that man downstairs at the window with a gun?" I roared at Fred.

I heard more running sounds coming from the driveway of our house.

I looked down to the floor, and there was my eldest son Roy, crouched down. He looked terrified. He moved toward my legs, put his arms around them, and squeezed. I touched his head and assured him it was going to be OK. The sound of sirens could be heard in a matter of minutes. Not too long after, there was a thunderous knocking on the downstairs door.

"It's the police! Open the door." More knocking and shouting came from the police until eventually Fred left the bathroom and went downstairs. Moments later there was a shout coming from the bottom of the stairs.

"Where are you, love? It's the police. It's OK. Everything is going to be OK now," an officer was assuring me. Minutes later my children and I were down in the sitting room along with Fred and numerous police officers. I heard a conversation taking place in the kitchen.

"We have searched the garden and found no one. The neighbours say two men went running down the road so we have people out looking now," came one voice.

"OK. Keep me up to date," said another officer. Moments later an officer came in through the front external door and asked Fred to accompany him to a waiting car. I looked out of the door from where I sat and I thought that I recognised that car." Fred looked straight at me, and the look on his face told me that I had to stay silent. Why? I had no idea. *This should not be happening. When will this crazy life return to normal? Please someone help us.* A police officer explained that a car would be coming shortly to escort me and my children from the property. The car arrived and I had no idea where I or my children were going. My eldest son Roy clung to me, petrified, and I could honestly relate to that feeling. I kept assuring him things were going to be OK. I didn't honestly believe what I was saying but I was this child's mother and he depended on me.

***

From inside a room in the police station, I heard voices in the corridor.

"Are we bringing Social Services?" a voice enquired.

"No, the super wants to handle this himself" was the reply. The door to the room opened. I was looking directly at the door. I had no idea what was going to happen. Everything seemed to be heightened.

"Is there anything I can get you" asked a man dressed in plain clothes.

"I want to go home with my children," I replied.

"That isn't going to happen any time soon. Is there anywhere else we can take you?" asked the man. Sometime later as my children and I were leaving the room I heard a noise, so I turned in the direction of where it was coming from. I recognised a man who was handcuffed; he was one of Fred's mates. No sooner had I seen him a door opened and there in front of me in the same direction was another man I recognised as one of Fred's mates. *Busy tonight.* I paused for a second. *Wait—why are these two men here?* The man in plain clothes tried to move me on in the direction he wanted me to go. I was rooted with dread. *I bet it was those men at our home tonight.* A sound came from the opposite direction; I turned to look, still not moving from the place where I stood. There stood Blondie, another one of Fred's mates who I had been introduced to a few weeks earlier. Then Silver walked out of a door which was in the opposite direction to us.

Another one. What was going on? The man in plain clothes started toward an exit door, holding my eldest son's hand. I followed.

Fifteen minutes later the children and I were at a friend's house; we had been expected. The whole house was awake, everyone looking to me for an answer. I gave none. The police instructed that the children and I were to stay at this house until later in the morning, when the police would come back and see us.

When the police returned later that morning they explained that they had been in contact with my mother and they were to move my children and me to my mother's house. I was told I had no say in the matter—the police were taking whatever steps they deemed safe, especially with the previous evening's events.

An hour later we were at my mother's house; shortly after a police officer of senior rank came knocking on my mother's door. I was informed that Fred had notified the police that the family car was missing. I was asked the details of my car. I told the officer what they wanted to know.

Chapter Five
Moving Counties

The council allocated a house to my family and me. I was trying to look ahead and forget the incidents of the past couple of weeks. I busied myself decorating the new house. I had been told that Fred had been mixed up in some sort of drug ring and he had tried to help the police secure conviction. Fred had said it was something that just happened, that he had no control over it, and he promised nothing like this would ever happen to us again. I had learned that Blondie and Silver were police officers, and I had been in too much contact with different ranking officers than I care to think about!

What was Fred's game? An investigating officer who was dealing with the incident at our previous home told me that I should consider not having anything to do with Fred anymore—otherwise I may end up in troubled waters. How could I not have anything to do with Fred? He was still threatening me with his previous crimes. I was so confused, I couldn't think straight. So much had happened in such a short space of time and just after the birth of my second son. I hadn't consented to any of this—everyone had made decisions for me and I was never asked for my own input about anything.

***

I was coming back to my mother's house, taking a shortcut across a field with my children. I looked up to see three men running in my direction from what appeared to be a car parked with its doors open at the side of the road. The men were shouting something. I was trying to make out what they were saying but didn't want to appear to be taking any notice of what they were saying. Before I knew it the three men were there in front of me; one picked up the pushchair containing my baby, one grabbed my eldest son and picked him up, while the other ordered that I needed to run as fast as I could and get in the car. They explained to me that they were police officers and they needed to get my children and me out of the area immediately.

"Why? Tell me what's wrong." I demanded to know.

"All will be explained later. Just hurry and get in the car!" one of the men said.

At the police station, I was told that the two men who had been arrested in relation to the gun incident at our previous home had turned up at my sister's house and subsequently the police had been called. At that time the two men were at large and it was now obvious they were hell-bent on finding Fred by whatever means. Our whereabouts had been confirmed to the police by my sister, so the police needed to have all three of us in protective custody. Blondie and Silver appeared at the police station and came to speak to me.

"How could you put me and my children in this situation?" I yelled. "What have we ever done to you? I want my life back and you have no right to involve me in this."

They told me it was an unforeseen incident that was getting out of hand and they had to take every necessary action to ensure we were safe. There was no two ways about it—we would have to move out of the county. There was no way we could stay where we were, and everyone had to think of the children. I was not happy at all. My life again was being taken from me but this time the police had an input.

***

We arrived in another county. We were given a home immediately, obviously something the police had put in place. Fred arrived later in the day. I had been told by the police that I must not under any circumstances contact any member of my family or friends because this could jeopardise our whereabouts and safety. I was furious at Fred and I let him know it. I was furious at the whole situation!

***

Over the following months I saw Blondie and Silver from a distance as they sat in a car outside our home. Fred would go sit in the car and speak to them. Each time I was told they were just updating Fred on the events that had happened in relation to the gun incident and the two men turning up at my sister's home.

One day I came downstairs to find Blondie and Silver in my sitting room. They were talking with Fred about a man named Michael Sams getting arrested for kidnapping and attempted murder. The man's latest crime had been that of kidnapping Stephanie Slater, an estate agent.

I found myself saying aloud, "Why are you here? and what has it got to

31

do with us that this man has been caught?" The room fell silent. Blondie and Silver made their excuses and left. Fred looked uncomfortable. I questioned his awkwardness, which turned into an argument. In a bid to reassure me nothing was wrong or he was up to something, Fred boasted that he had entrapped Blondie and Silver and went onto say neither knew it yet but they soon would. That was his little safe keeping, and I had nothing to worry about. Fred left the house.

What had he meant? What had he done to Blondie and Silver? What was he up to now?

Later that day I tried to bring the earlier conversation back up, but Fred wouldn't divulge anything. That led to further arguments and I finally snapped. I threw everything I could think of at him verbally. He was in no doubt of how I felt about things.

Over the coming weeks and months I saw nothing more of Blondie or Silver, and my distance became greater with Fred. I hated the sight of him. I dreaded him coming in when he went out and going out when he was in. Nothing was acceptable to me, and I hated being away from my home county. I was trapped, and Fred ensured when we did speak that he hadn't forgotten his threat towards me.

Chapter Six
Fred's Antics with New Control

Within a month or so I had realised that Fred had a new plaything—a girlfriend. It was someone I had met many years earlier. She was a part-time prostitute.

They are suited to each other! I studied how Fred's behaviour changed, and it made me laugh. The way Fred lied, behaviour, and explanations came out, was like watching a child trying to see how far they could push the boundaries before the parent would put a stop to such actions. The thing that made me curious about their relationship was why would a part-time prostitute want to be involved in such a loser like Fred? And vice versa. It didn't make sense to me, but there was obviously something that drew them together and maybe one day I would find out what it was. Apart from the curiosity, I didn't give a damn about their relationship. She was welcome to him. I would have even gift wrapped him if she would have asked. I knew that I had to get away from Fred and the whole situation. The only hesitation I had about our departure was where would the children and I go? There was no way we could return back to the South Yorkshire area where my family lived. That had been made perfectly clear by the police when we had all been removed. This really infuriated me. That trapped feeling was unbearable. There was no way I could go to my family for help. Apart from the danger they would be put in if I was to go back to South Yorkshire, I also would receive a lot of questions from everyone. I was finding it hard to cope with everything that had happened and couldn't put the feelings into words. Things that had happened during my relationship with Fred only really happened in movies, I had thought. But no—it had happened to my children and me. The worst thing about it was that the police had been at the back of what had happened at our home address in the South Yorkshire area and I had never been consulted if I wanted us to be involved in their actions and plans! How could the people we are taught to respect in authority treat us like this? How could I answer all the questions my family would have? I was finding it hard to think about what had happened, let alone talk about it. Then the suspicious side of certain family members made it a definite no because I knew what sort of people they were and knew what sort of action they would more than likely take. I didn't want that sort of behaviour and outcome playing on my conscience on top of everything else.

I was just hoping that Fred would announce his departure from the family unit so that I could move forward with our lives somehow and make a new start somewhere where no one would know us or anything that Fred and the police had done to us. I was always going to miss my mum and wished I could sit and talk to her, but the way things were there was no way that was going to happen soon. I knew that my mother would be anxious and want to know that my children and I were OK. I could understand how she must have been feeling. I was a mother myself, and all parents would want to know if their child and grand children are all right, especially when they just disappeared in the manner we had. I thought of my mother often and hoped one day I would be able to tell her everything once I had sorted what Fred had done while I had been with him. If there was one person in the world I could trust it would be my mum, but I couldn't even trust myself and the way I had been acting over the time I had been with Fred—keeping silent and allowing someone to have this fearful hold over me. Why couldn't I just speak out? I couldn't because I knew Fred would carry out his threats as he had so many times when other people had crossed him, and I had seen for myself what treatment they had received at his hands. Knowing my mother and how she would have responded was another thing that made me fear telling her. She was very direct and didn't mince her words and there was no doubt she would have gone straight to the top of the police force and someone would have got what for, so to speak. But knowing Fred he would somehow make that backfire on me and I didn't feel able to cope, especially with going to prison. I had not asked to be a part of any crime and I didn't want to be seen as a criminal either.

***

One day Fred and the prostitute were sat in the living room talking. I was in the kitchen but I could hear snippets of the conversation they were having in the room.

"Do you think she will pay up?" Fred asked.

"Yes. She is a bossy old cow and she loves centre light. She will because it's her grandson. Then we will nearly have enough," said the prostitute.

The voices hushed as I deliberately made my presence known. Entering the living room they changed direction in conversation as to not alert me to the fact that they were scheming something. This was unusual for Fred. He usually made sure I knew what he was doing in a roundabout way, but not this time. He hadn't told me of any evil thing he had planned or was going to do with the prostitutes.

That got me thinking two things about Fred. Either he would leave, as I wanted him to, or he was having this prostitute over good style. To be honest I hoped it was both. Fred felt uncomfortable speaking in my presence and I suppose I wasn't making it easy for him because I sat there just looking at him and not saying a word. I had recently learned he hated me looking directly at him and not saying a word. I loved the way this rattled him slightly but not to any significant degree where his crime was concerned; he still committed them. It just made him keep moving out of my eyesight usually, and the only time it had ever had some sort of impact was when he was entertaining his criminal friends and I wouldn't speak to him—I'd just look. I felt that I had to adapt my behaviour slightly to get maximum impact, to make him feel he wasn't in control anymore, but I hadn't got that far yet.

Fred and the prostitute made their excuses and left the house. I had no idea of where they were going and I didn't care. What I did know was I hoped in my heart that whatever they were up to they would get caught.

***

After catching little bits of conversations over the following weeks I felt it was time to confront Fred about the small son of his prostitute girlfriend. I had gathered that whatever the two had going, it had something to do with him. Her son had disappeared from her care and I thought it was strange how she hadn't been contacting the child's father as she had done many times over the weeks on my phone. I'd gotten my opportunity, just Fred and I in the house alone. I approached him with contempt.

"Na then, now is the time to answer some questions." I said, staring straight into his eyes.

"What?"

"What's going off with your girlfriend's son? Don't try denying it! I'm not stupid! So come on—what's happening?" I asked.

"Nothing! And it's got nothing to do with you! You just concentrate on looking after the kids and the house," he answered, acting all cocky, as he did when he was up to something.

"Well, one day it will come out and God help you if it's anything wicked toward that boy!" I growled at him.

"Bollocks, and don't you be going looking for something that isn't there!

35

What I do is my business so stay out of it," he snarled back at me.

From that reaction I knew I had hit the nail on the head. It was definitely something wrong toward this boy, but I would have to wait until it came out, as things usually did.

A few days later the police came by to arrest Fred. I thought, "Now I will find out what he's done in relation to this boy," but I was wrong. The police had come to arrest him on charges of fraud and deception, his usual activity. He was detained in custody and sent on remand to prison pending further investigations. A week or so passed and I went to the prison to see Fred. I hadn't seen the girlfriend and that was unusual because she usual serviced men in the area where we all lived.

"So where's the girlfriend?" I asked Fred.

"She is not my girlfriend! I was just out making money through her, that's all," he replied. "Anyway, let's not talk about her. What have you and the kids been up to? I hear through the grapevine that you have had quite a few visitors while I have been in here! So what's the word?" Fred asked, looking straight at me.

"You what? Who says I have had visitors? Visitors? Why would I want anything to do with the shitheads you associate with? No one has been to see me and the kids. We sit in our prison where you put us. Unable to communicate with the outside world. You bastard! Is the girlfriend winding you up? Even when you're not there it appears that the kids and I can't attempt a bit of peace! Tell your girlfriend to go fuck herself and if she has a problem tell her to come and see me, you twat!" My voice was raising and everyone was looking at our table in the visiting room.

"What you fucking looking at? Don't you ever row?" I shouted in the direction of a crowd of people sat at a table close by.

They all looked away.

"It isn't her! It doesn't matter what you do or where you go, I will always know where you are. Don't think because I'm in here I don't know things because if you do you are sadly mistaken. I know your every move—don't ever forget that." Fred grinned at me in his evil way.

"How's about bollocks! I do what I want when I want whenever I want, and no one owns me! Do you hear that?" I growled back at him.

Leaning across the table Fred said, "Listen here. I've always told you don't ever think that you will escape me because you won't! You think now you can do what you want, but at any given time I will have you off the streets and away from the kids and you will never see them again."

I saw the pure evilness in his face.

Fred then went onto say, "Oh, and I will tell you this—don't think I care about the kids because I don't. I sold that son of hers! That little boy and I didn't give a fuck! Fucking women! Who needs them?" He was so arrogant when he said it.

"You sold her son? Who to?" I asked, horrified at what he had just said.

He ignored my question. "So as I say, don't think I won't do what I say. You will always be with me no matter where you are!" Fred grinned at me.

"Bollocks, You bastard! What have you done with this boy? You are an evil bastard! You and your girlfriend deserve each other! I will find out, I'm telling you!" I was furious.

"I will just make sure that my friends don't listen to anything you say. They hate you and your family. They would never accept anything you say," Fred said looking straight into my eyes.

He meant every word. I had seen that look so many times. I had seen several victims suffer when he had threatened to do something to them with that exact look in his eye. I knew he would not hesitate if he had to do something to keep me where he had me. I sat there for a few moments just looking at him. I could see it was getting to him. He was waiting for me to say something, but I just remained quiet. I just kept staring at him. The atmosphere between us was electrifying. Then without warning Fred jumped up out of his chair and said, "We have nothing further to talk about. You just remember what I've said!" and he started walking off the visit.

"You're an evil bastard and one day you will get what's coming to you!" I shouted after him as he made his way toward the officers to let him out of the visiting room.

"What you lot looking at?" I growled at everyone who was staring. I made my way out of the visiting room.

On the way home on the train I played everything over in my head. "What had he meant by he had sold the girlfriend's son?" Terrible thoughts of child abuse were going through my head. I felt ill. I knew there was nothing I could do about reporting what Fred had told me. First, there were his police friends. He had told me that they wouldn't listen. Second, I didn't have enough information about the girlfriend's son to even get someone in authority to take a look into what I suspected. I decided that when I got home I would go see someone I knew the girlfriend serviced on a regular basis and ask him to help me try and find out any information about the son. I didn't know how I was going to approach the person, but I had to do something.

When I arrived at the house the person I had gone to see wasn't in so I thought I would call back later.

I arrived home at tea time. My children were hungry and demanding their supper. I had started cooking when the phone rang.

"Hello," I answered the call.

"Don't you forget what you have been told." said Fred.

"Bollocks!" and I put the phone down on him.

After tea a friend of my neighbour knocked on the window as he was passing. I looked up and acknowledged him by nodding my head. About half hour went past and the neighbour and his friend knocked on the door.

"Hello duck, we thought we would call for a cuppa. We have heard that his Lordship is locked up. How is he? Is that where you have been today?" the neighbour asked.

"Do I really have to speak about him?" I asked sarcastically.

During the course of the visit I started asking the neighbour about Fred's girlfriend's son and tried to get some information that might help me if I went to the authorities. I got nothing that I didn't already know, so that had been a wasted exercise.

***

A few weeks passed and Fred got bail while the police were still carrying out there enquiries. It wasn't that long before Fred was back to his usual self. He started taking things from the house that had a little bit of value. He sold them and kept the money for whatever he needed it for. He stole money out of my purse that I needed to feed the children and keep the house warm. As usual, his needs came first. The girlfriend was back on the scene within a couple of days. It was business as usual for them.

Chapter Seven
Theft of the Post Bag

I had many violent arguments with Fred. Numerous times I told him I wish he'd die. I hated living in the same house as him. I hated the sight of him and wished I could just get away from him. He had a hold over me and I hated it. I had seen over the time that I had been involved in the relationship with him that when he said he was going to do something he always did it, no matter what the cost. One morning I lay awake; my children were both asleep and there seemed no need to get up early, so I rested while I could. Rest was something that I had learned to go without over a period of time. I was waiting, always waiting for something to happen because it always did, of that I could be sure.

"Wake up! Wake up!" Fred was rocking me to get my attention.

"What? Get off me! Fuck off and leave me alone!" I growled back at him.

"You need to get up! Quick come downstairs!" And Fred was gone.

Minutes later I entered the sitting room, where I heard ripping noises. What met me stunned me.

"What the...?" I went to say.

"Shut up—this is our future," Fred ordered.

"No! No! I'm having nothing to do with this. You're mad and need locking up," I yelled at Fred.

Within a second he was on top of me, pushing me down on the sofa.

"Shut up. I've told you I'm the boss here and there will never be anyway you will escape me. Get used to it—what I do so do you"! Fred grimaced through his teeth at me. There in the middle of the room was a pile of paper and envelopes. Unopened letters stood in a mountain in the middle of the sitting room. There among the pile was a post bag. Thoughts immediately started rushing through my mind. I saw images of guns, violence, and crime no right-minded person would ever do to another human being.

I found herself saying aloud, "Please God, don't let anyone be hurt. I beg you."

"Shut up, woman, and get this paper in these bags!" Fred barked.

"No! No! I will have nothing to do with this. I hate you. I wish they would catch you. You deserve to be shot to death. You're an evil bastard"! I grimaced through my teeth at him.

Immediately he was there again, holding me down on the sofa. I felt his hands around my throat, tightening.

"Listen here—get used to the idea you will never be rid of me and the sooner you accept that the easier life will be," he said. Suddenly the sitting room door opened, and in walked a young boy, Rowan, who had been rescued from his violent father and was now residing with us.

"Oh no—don't tell me your involved in this?" I blurted out.

"Yes, I'm going to be rich now," said the young lad. Immediately I was transported back in time to the pit yard. The adolescence boy, his cries for his mother, the gun. The hold Fred had over the boy and me. Fred was merciless. Here we were again in a similar situation—another child, another serious crime—and I felt helpless. I looked at Fred.

"You are nothing but a bastard! How dare you? Again! A child, you bastard," I screamed at him.

Fred immediately sprang at me.

"Shut your mouth! I've told you before—we do as I say."

Rowan laughed to himself. I was helpless; another child was being led to the slaughterhouse and he hadn't a clue what he was getting involved in. I pushed Fred from me.

"Your nothing but a bastard, and don't think I'm having anything to do with it!" I growled at Fred as I was leaving the room. I turned to the boy Rowan and said in a pleading tone, "Go home, Rowan, before it's too late! Get away from here now while you can." The non action showed me that the Rowan was hooked and his life would also be ruined; I had no way of saving him. Fred preyed on young boys, of that now I was sure. I wondered what else had happened to Rowan while he had been involved in Fred's life. Something must have. I was sure of that, but what? That one was anyone's guess. What I now knew in my heart was that Rowan was lost. I felt ill. I made my way back upstairs and just wanted to go to sleep in the hope that when I awoke this would all have been some bad dream. Minutes passed. I heard the outside door shut. I was out of bed in a flash and making my way to the window. Moments later I saw Rowan with two sacks over his back, one on each shoulder, making his was across the field.

"Silly boy, you have no idea," I said out loud. My children were still sleeping as I watched

Rowan continued walking, fading in the distance.

Within half an hour Rowan was back and sat downstairs. The children had woken and I had no choice but to go downstairs and be in the same room as Fred.

"It won't be long now and they will be here." Fred was talking to Rowan.

"Well, they won't find anything, so fuck them." Rowan grinned.

No sooner had that been said there was a loud knocking at the door. Within seconds the police had gained entry. All three of us—Fred, Rowan, and I—were then transported to the local police station. The children were left with a neighbour I hardly knew. We were all released on bail pending further enquiries. Upon my release and back at home with Fred and Rowan I informed Fred that I had been told that Rowan had been pinching Royal Mail, and I wanted to know if it was true. Neither of them admitted it, but there must have been something in what the police had told me. This would have been something Fred would have got the lad to do—I just knew it.

Chapter Eight
Fred Sets the Scene

Over the coming days things in the house started to take a turn. I told Fred that I was going to leave and I was taking the children with me. At that stage I couldn't care less what Fred threatened to do or what he was going to do to me. Fred realised that I meant business. I couldn't take the pressure any more. Against all my conditioning, I didn't care what happened to me; I was leaving. Fred walked across the room, picked up the baby, made his way upstairs, and shouted to my eldest child to come upstairs. I was fuming still and adamant I was leaving. I heard the dragging of something across the floor upstairs. After a few minutes I went upstairs to see what all the noise was about. All doors on the landing were shut. Where were they? I walked to my bedroom door first; I tried the handle, and the door wouldn't open.

"Open this door now! Why is the door shut fast?" I yelled through the door.

Suddenly I heard Fred shouting. "Help! Help! She is going to kill us. Someone call the police," his cries continued.

"Open this door now or I will break it down," I threatened.

I heard muffled voices outside. *Who was he talking to? What was being said? What was the crazy idiot doing in the bedroom with my children?*

"Open this door now! I mean it! Open it!" I yelled at Fred through the door.

I heard the downstairs door open, then a voice.

"What's up? What's happened?" Rowan who lived with us shouted up the stairs.

I walked to the top of the stairs, looking down at Rowan; I suddenly heard the door on my bedroom open. There stood Fred waving a long-handled knife at me.

"You're trying to kill us," he gibed.

Before I had time to respond my eldest son, peeping through the door, said, "Yes you are, and we will tell the police when they arrive."

"Oh no, please God, not my boy! Please no!" I said.

Fred slammed the door shut to the bedroom. I pulled and thumped at the door, yelling for the door to be open. I couldn't imagine what Fred had told my eldest son. Why had he, my son Roy, said those things? How had this happened? I had never seen this coming. My son was falsely saying incriminating things to my face. What the fuck?

Throughout the rest of that day I was between the sitting room and the upstairs landing, yelling at Fred to open the door. Fred was having none of it. During the course of the day I thought surely he will come out of the bedroom soon. I wondered how he could stay in that room with no water or food for either of my children, and then it hit me. Somehow he was getting food and water, but surely he hadn't had the time to get these things into that room. This situation had happened so fast. I again heard low voices coming from outside the house. I went downstairs and to the back door, and there in front of me was our next-door neighbour and Rowan that lived with us attaching to a rope a box. I discovered when I opened it that it contained drinks and food. How dare the neighbour do this? Rowan was just a boy, but that was a snapping point for me. I launched a full assault on the neighbour. I lost my temper and the next thing I knew Fred was there dragging me off the neighbour and dragging me inside the house.

"Try leaving me will you? People now know what a nutcase you are, and even your son has told them you're dangerous. Do you think anyone will ever believe a thing you say? Forget it—because they won't," He spat his words at me.

Chapter Nine
Murder of a Postman

In the early 1990's Fred had again been put on remand to prison while police carried out their investigation of the charges he faced.

Fred was due to appear before the local magistrate's court, and he had sent instruction to me through his friends that I should attend on the morning in question so that I would be able to have a visit after the court hearing because he didn't intend to apply for bail at the hearing and I hadn't been to the prison for a few week to see him.

I arrived at the court with the Rowan that lived with me and my children. We entered the courtroom and waited for Fred to be brought before the courts for the hearing. There was no way of knowing what time he would appear, so it was just a waiting game. We sat watching other people being brought before the courts on various charges.

"I'm hungry," said Rowan.

I reached into my bag and took some money from my purse.

"Here. Go to the sandwich shop at the end of the path outside the courthouse. Bring me a sandwich too please," I said, handing the lad a bank note.

As the lad was checking the order for the shop with me I noticed a group of middle-aged men entering the courtroom. They seemed to be looking in the direction of both Rowan and me. Rowan sensed that I was staring at something, so he turned to look.

"Who the fuck are they?" he asked me.

"I haven't got a clue, but they look like undercover police officers and they definitely want us to know they're sat there," I replied.

Rowan set off for the sandwiches while I sat in the courtroom waiting for Fred to be brought before the court. About ten minutes later Fred was brought before the court and I thought, "Well Rowan can come on the visit even though he will miss the hearing."

I heard Fred coming up the steps toward the court room. As he entered the room from below, he looked to see where I was and then he looked over to where this group of men where sat. While looking at the group of men, for a moment he seemed to raise his head in acknowledgment to them. I thought, "They are definitely police officers and they are going down to the cells to see Fred after the court hearing."

I wondered where the lad had got to because he had been gone a while. The court hearing lasted at the most five minutes, and Fred was remanded in custody pending further enquiries by the police. As Fred left the courtroom he looked again toward the group of men and then at me. He gave me a smile as he was led down the stairs in the dock to the cell area beneath the courtroom. I stood up to make my way to the door. I wanted to find out where Rowan was, then go to the cell area of the court building to ask if we could have a short visit with Fred. As I was leaving the court-room I could feel these men looking at me with what I could only describe as menacing stares. I stopped in my tracks and looked directly at them.

"What you staring at? Do I owe you something?" I asked.

Within a second I was pushed out of the courtroom and tackled to the floor by some of these men. I fought back, lashing out with my arms and feet, but I had no chance. Then the next thing I knew I was placed in handcuffs as I lay face down on the floor.

I was dragged to my feet and I just heard a few words from a man who was stood in front of me.

Arrest, murder, Sheffield. Before I knew it I was being dragged toward a flight of stairs in the waiting area inside the courthouse. The entire area had fallen silent and everyone was looking in our direction. I heard the same man say something.

I heard, "We will show you! You will get life for this! Think you're a hard nut?" It was just words that were a blur to me. I was placed in a police car that had been pulled up to the doors where the cells beneath the court were.

At the police station I was questioned about the murder of a Sheffield postman who had been killed by someone while he was at a post box emptying it of the daily contents. Someone had run over the postman with his own van and as a result the postman had died.

"So, why have you arrested me?" I asked the officers.

"Because more than two hundred people have phoned the enquiry line and put your name forward," an officer answered my question.

"I don't even know that amount of people," I replied.

The interview went on with the two interviewing officers continuing to ask, "Why would so many people phone in and give your name if you had nothing to do with the murder?"

I told the officer they must have really been struggling to find the responsible person for this crime to come and arrest a mother of two children who just stays in her home with her kids only to leave for vital things to keep the house ticking over. I was sat there thinking I could remember the day it had been reported on the TV news that the postman had been killed. That date I had been to parents' evening at school for my eldest son, Roy. Later that night on the local news the death had been reported. So I told the officers of my whereabouts and one of them said to me, "Yeah, like fuck! Don't think we won't get you for this murder because we will. You really think you're a someone but we will show you." I was later let out on bail pending further enquiries, and I was given a date and time to attend back at the police station. I discovered on my release that Rowan had been arrested too. He had been told the same as me, that 200 people had called the enquiry line and given our names.

Chapter Ten
It Was Always the Weak Ones

During the time that we lived in the Derbyshire area Fred's behaviour became more aggressive and open. He attacked various people, all in the same way. To Fred, it didn't matter how old the victim was as long as he got what he wanted, and that was usually money so he could feed his gambling addiction. We hadn't been living at our home long when he came home saying that one of the prostitute's clients was an idiot and he was going to take his house off him. I had no idea how, why, or when he was going to do that, but I did know he meant what he said. I didn't understand why he was telling me what he was going to do because there was nothing I could have done to stop him doing whatever he wanted. I believed it was to make me suffer. To me there was no other explanation.

**

One day around tea time Fred came back to our home with the girlfriend and a man in tow. I immediately thought, "Bet this is the next victim!" I was right. After all three had been in the house an hour or so I saw straight through what Fred was doing. He was winning this young man over and abstracting information from him about his financial status. The girlfriend picked up conversations where he left off. I just carried on around the house doing what I always did—chores. A few times Fred had tried to engage me in their conversation but I didn't reply so he quickly covered over his embarrassment with his continued flow of conversation. I saw the young man look and frown at me because I never answered anything that was asked of me. But I knew something he didn't know, and as soon as I got any chance I was going to get the message to this young man that he must never have anything to do with either of these two people he was sat trusting his personal information with. I knew he probably wouldn't believe me, but I had to try. It was after a few more visits to our home that I got the chance to tell him to get away from them. This was how I approached the subject.

"I don't speak often and I have my reasons. You don't know me and I don't know you, but please listen when I say that you need to stop associating with these two. Fred is a very dangerous person and so is the woman you think loves you. If I were you I would get as far away as possible and as quickly as possible." I could tell the young man didn't know what to make of my warning, but time would tell if he had heeded it.

***

Over the coming weeks Fred and the girlfriend would boast how they had taken this young man's wages and fobbed him off with nothing but a load of lies as to how they were using his money. The time had come around for the young man's mortgage to be paid. He had turned up at the door asking Fred when he was going to see some return for his investment. Fred fobbed him off again, and the following month the young man was back asking the same all over again. I just sat taking in all that was said.

"You will have to come to the pub tonight and I will give you it then," said Fred.

The young man left, saying he would see him later in the pub. In the meantime another one of Fred's associates had been contacted by Fred, and he asked the associate to make sure the young man never asked about his money again. The associate agreed. I didn't know how they were going to stop him, but I knew something was going to happen. The evening came around and Fred left for the pub. This was unusual for Fred because he wasn't one for pubs. So I'd gathered things must have been quite serious for him to frequent a pub, especially at night.

It wasn't long before Fred and the associate returned to our house. I was upstairs bathing the children and I could hear roars of laughter coming from the sitting room. After getting the children into bed and settled I went into the sitting room, and there it was described to me how the associate had punched and broken the young man's jaw and he had been taken to hospital. They thought they deserved a badge of honour for their actions! I just sat there feeling numb. I had done all I could to protect this young man from them, but obviously the young man thought he knew best.

After a few days the young man turned up with Fred's girlfriend. His jaw had been wired up and he had had an emergency operation on his jaw while in hospital. Fred's girlfriend left the house for a while and the young man came in the kitchen where I was ironing. He handed me a piece of paper. I read it and it said that he wished he had listened to me and he couldn't get out of their clutches. He wrote that they had been at his home every night when he had returned from work and they took every penny he had. He explained that Fred had always said that he could come to our house for tea on a night as long as he handed over his money to Fred. He wrote that he had been made to feel that he had to give them money. I hadn't finished reading what had been put on the paper when Fred's girlfriend returned. I put the paper under the pile of clothes and thought that I didn't really need to read any further I could imagine. Fred and the girlfriend were in the kitchen later that night having a cuppa, so the young man was alone briefly. I turned to him and spoke quietly.

"Get away now! Tonight. Go anywhere and don't ever come back, promise me?" I said to him.

The young man nodded.

"Make sure you never come back because they will never leave you alone. Take it from me—I am not kidding. There must be somewhere that they don't know about where you can be safe. She is just as bad as him, so don't be fooled by her," I said.

I left the room before Fred and his girlfriend came back and hoped the young man would somehow make his excuses and get away from them as quickly as possible.

Later that night the girlfriend phoned Fred. From the conversation I gathered the young man had made his excuses and she had left him at his address, saying she would see him the following morning.

Good. And God keep you safe.

Morning came around soon enough and I was awoken by Fred shouting at someone. I went downstairs, and the girlfriend was stood taking a right tongue lashing from Fred. It appeared that she had first gone to the young man's house and couldn't get an answer from the young man so she had phoned Fred, knowing he would be up. Then he had gone to the young man's house and he couldn't get a reply either. Fred was furious, saying the young man had never done anything like this before so she must have alerted him to their plan. The girlfriend was denying anything to do with his disappearance.

"Did he say anything to you when he was sat with you last night?" Fred asked me.

"Bollocks." I looked him dead in the eye. He knew I meant what I was saying and he knew he wouldn't get anything out of me when I answered in that tone. What I did know was that I would be paid back by Fred for letting me talk to him like that. But as long as the young man was safe, it wouldn't be something I hadn't experienced with Fred before.

***

A few days had passed and Fred and the girlfriend had discovered that the young man was down in the Birmingham area. They were making plans to go see him with the intention of bringing him back into their claws. They left, and I hoped the young man wouldn't be found. A few hours later they were back. I gathered from their conversation they had located the lad at his father's public house and they had not been able to get him on his own. They were frustrated but still planned to return and fetch him back. It never happened; they never managed to get him to come back to his house.

Chapter Eleven
Kidnapping

I had visited the doctor's surgery with my youngest son. I was just leaving the surgery when Fred appeared in the doorway.

"Come on—hurry up! I've been looking for you everywhere!" Fred barked in an annoyed voice.

"What do you want? I don't have to tell you where I'm going and you know anyway that the baby is ill," I barked back.

"Shut up and get in the car. We have somewhere we need to go," he replied sharply.

I was not aware of any appointments that I needed to keep other than the one I had just attended. Fred was making a scene outside the surgery, so to shut him up I got in the car with the baby. Sat in the front seat was Fred's girlfriend. I never said anything—just sat there with the baby as Fred drove the car. He was telling me that he knew where our car was—the one that had been stolen from us at our previous address.

"So we are going to get the car back, and that's why I was trying to find you. I can't drive two cars back, can I"? Fred asked me.

"What, and you think I'm going to? Because I don't think so! I have the baby and no chair. How come you have found the car, and why don't you just call the police and tell them?" I spat at him.

Within twenty minutes or so, the car we were travelling in came to a halt.

"Right. I won't be a minute. Stay here!" Fred disappeared down the road on foot.

Within five minutes he was on his way back to the car.

"Can you just come and explain to this man about how our car was stolen and has been reported as stolen because he doesn't believe me. I've told him I'm having my car back and it's something he will have to accept because I am not leaving here without it. I've told him to call the police in this area, but I'm still having my car back." Fred was annoyed.

"No, I'm not going. I've told you to phone the police," I replied.

Within a second Fred was leading me by the arm and down a drive to someone's house. Inside the house were a couple and Fred immediately started saying to them both it was his car and it had been stolen. He asked the man, "Have you called the police?"

He replied, "Yes, but no one is picking up the phone."

Minutes later Fred, the man with our stolen car, and I came out from the man's drive, and Fred was telling the man he should follow him to the man's local police station.

I had this dreadful feeling inside, I sensed something was going to happen and there would be trouble.

A few minutes later we were parked outside a subdivision police station that obviously wasn't manned twenty-four hours a day.

Fred and the man both got back into the separate cars, and Fred stated that they were going to another police station. The car came to a halt at a police station in the Derbyshire area. Fred and the man went inside. About five minutes later they came out and Fred was telling the man to follow him again. Fred got in the car and said, "They are not on duty." Obviously he had gone to see someone he knew. In the car the baby had thrown up all over me and we were only a matter of minutes away from where we lived. Fred said he would take me home and I could sort myself and the baby out. He made me believe he would be going elsewhere once the baby and I had been dropped off. But when we got to our home Fred asked the man if he would come inside while he tried to contact the police officers who were aware of the circumstances surrounding the theft of the car.

A minute later both the baby and I were upstairs getting a shower and changing our clothes. When I had finished I went downstairs with the baby and entered the sitting room, from where raised voices were coming.

"Go on, give it him, the bastard!" growled Fred's girlfriend.

I turned toward the direction in which she was looking. Fred had the man pinned down on the settee with a knife to his throat (the same one he had in the bedroom and had waved at me).

"No! Don't do that!" I yelled as I ran at Fred in an attempt to get him off the man.

"Go on, cut the bastard's throat!" growled the girlfriend.

"No! No! No!" I was pulling at Fred to get him off the man. Fred had lost it; he was in a right temper but I could not stand and watch this happen. I wanted no part of it.

Fred let go of the man, but he was still threatening to harm him. The man sat up, Fred barking at him that he should go down to the car, empty it of everything that belonged to him, then bring the keys back to him. The man rose from the settee and walked toward the sitting room door.

"And if you're thinking of running away, don't. Don't forget I know where you live." Fred spat the words at the man. There was no mistaking Fred meant every word he said.

Fred handed the man a bag to put his belongings in.

"You bastard! How could you? And here in this house! You're a mad man," I screamed at him.

"You should have let him have it!" said Fred's girlfriend, as though what he had done would get him some sort of badge of honour.

I turned to look at her, and in an instant Fred had hold of me.

"I've told you we do as I say."

Fred let go of my arm and I walked to the window to look out. To my amazement the man was emptying the car. I wished at him telepathically, "Run, mister, run!"

The man emptied the car and came back to the house. I couldn't believe it. *Was this man daft?* Fred took the keys from the man and told him he would take him and drop him off at the bus station and he would give him his bus fare to get home. The man agreed. The man stood there on the outside landing waiting for everyone to get ready to go in the car.

"I'm staying here," I said.

"No, you're not! You're coming for the ride," Fred ordered.

Minutes later all five of us were in the car, Fred driving to the bus station where he handed the man a bank note for his bus fare to get home.

Back on our way home, Fred thought his actions were world class and the girlfriend was agreeing with him. They were saying things like, "Result! He was a Muppet! They would never have handed over the car!"

I sat in the back of the car silent with the baby. I couldn't comprehend what had just happened.

Why didn't the man run away as soon as he had got out of the house? I would have.

Why hadn't he tried to get someone's attention while he was out alone on the street? I would have!

Why had he taken the money for bus fare from Fred? I would have legged it! These things were going through my head.

Here was a man of average build and he obviously was intimidated by

Fred, just as I was. The man obviously believed that Fred would carry out his threats; he had meant everything he had said and done. The way Fred manipulated everyone made it very difficult to not do what he was telling you. There was this look in his eyes.

***

We arrived back home. Fred was in a happy mood, and his girlfriend was too. Fred and the girlfriend were talking about her next client, whose appointment she had to keep and it was just an hour away from the time. She was a part-time call girl, but she and Fred made a small living from her job. Fred ordered that I should take the girlfriend to her brother's house because she needed to collect something before she went to the appointment. I had tried to refuse, but I knew Fred's look all too well by this stage of our relationship. The girlfriend and I left the house. As we turned the corner on the landing to exit the external stairs we were met with police officers.

"You're under arrest! You have the right to remain silent! Anything you say may or can be used as evidence against you."

I was face down on the ground. I sensed that the girlfriend was nearby and believed she had been arrested. I was dragged to a waiting police car. Handcuffed and hurting I was thrown into the waiting car. The car sped off at high speed. I arrived at the police station where I was produced at the charge desk. While I was being booked in I heard a noise behind me and I turned. It was Fred; he too had been arrested. I was placed in a detention room and advised that someone would be in shortly to interview me.

Hours passed, and then the door opened.

"Come on. Get up. You are moving to another police station," an officer said.

"Another police station? Why?" I asked.

"Because this crime was not reported at this police station so you are being taken to the station that is dealing with the complaint," the officer said.

Minutes later I was en route to a police station in the south Yorkshire region. When I arrived I was produced again at the charge desk. I heard the words kidnap, threats to kill, blackmail and taken without owner's consent.

"Me?" I asked, looking at the officers.

"Yes, you" came their reply.

***

As the days passed and I was interviewed I realised that the girlfriend hadn't been arrested. The man had told the police that his wife had been the one encouraging the attack upon him. I had been told nothing about my children when I enquired over them.

Days passed and eventually both Fred and I were brought before the courts. I was let out on bail and Fred was remanded. I could talk to no one about how Fred was conducting himself or that I had not been the person encouraging the attack and hadn't even known where the car was. I was an innocent party to all of this. The police had told me I was the one who made Fred commit crimes and I was the mastermind behind every crime he had committed while he had lived with me.

I knew none of this was true, but who was I to say anything, especially to the police, who obviously had their own opinion? In the past I had tried to say I wasn't guilty of the crimes I had been arrested for and, like every criminal I was told, "They all say that!"

***

Over the coming months while I was on bail I came across the girlfriend. When she realised it was me she ran into a shop for protection. She was doing everything she could to avoid me. Later that same day the police visited me, saying that they had received a complaint from a witness in the upcoming court case. That's when I realised the girlfriend had not been charged and I was facing charges that I had nothing to do with other than be an innocent person in the wrong place at the wrong time. She was a witness and she was the guilty party. What a joke!

***

The case eventually came to court and the girlfriend gave evidence against both Fred and me. Sentences were passed; I was set free while Fred was sentenced to three years in prison.

Chapter Twelve
Mrs. Rat

With Fred being detained at her Majesty's pleasure I had to move house on my own. We were moving about three miles away from our present home where the police had put us when we had been moved from our home county. The house had been offered to our family unit by the local council.

Before Fred had been incarcerated he had paid someone he knew to rearrange the bathroom in the new property. Unfortunately for us, this person had been arrested and was detained at her Majesty's pleasure too. So the house needed repairs to make the bathroom functional. I had no money and was living on benefit so I couldn't pay for a plasterer, and there would be no way the council would repair the wall because when the house had been offered to us it was in fit repair.

***

The day of the move came. I had packed everything and I had to go with the children to a local van rental business and hire a self-drive van to enable us to move. We arrived around lunch time. I asked Rowan who lived with us to entertain my children while I got the beds up and bedding put on them so at least we could we could rest properly that evening. Rowan and Roy were out in the back garden playing with a ball. I was upstairs in the new property when I heard Roy crying. I immediately went downstairs to see what the problem was. I went through the door to exit the house and there was the Rowan engaged in a shouting match with one of the neighbours. They were having a right go at each other, and within a second I was stood beside Rowan and Roy. It transpired that the ball had gone into their garden and the new neighbour was hell-bent on not returning the ball to its rightful owner.

"Now then, return that ball." I looked the new neighbour straight in the eye.

"No way! You are not having this ball. It is in my garden and I'm keeping it! They shouldn't be playing in the garden with a ball, so I'm not returning it," Mrs. Rat growled.

I moved forward nearer to the fence that divided the two properties.

"I'll ask you again to give that ball back," I went on to say, "There is nothing in my contract with the local council that says that my children cannot play ball on the garden, and if you don't return it I will have no choice but to phone the police because that ball belongs to my son. Now please return it!"

Mrs. Rat was having none of the sense I was saying. She turned on her heels and went into her home and slammed the door behind her.

In an instant I jumped over the fence and was knocking on her door. She wouldn't answer it. I stood there a few moments and then I lifted the letter box and started speaking into it.

"Now, missus, I don't know what your problem is but I just want our ball back." I stood there listening to see if she would reply. She didn't, so I continued to talk into the letter box. After a few more minutes I walked away and came back to Roy, Rowan and Reggie my baby in his pushchair. Obviously Roy wasn't happy that he hadn't got his ball back but until I could speak to Mrs. Rat and appeal to her conscious I couldn't retrieve the ball. We all went in the house.

While putting things into the cabinet that was in the room I saw the ball come back over the fence. Someone had obviously seen sense and agreed the ball was our property.

***

The following day I was still unpacking everything and Roy was again playing in our back garden. I heard someone shouting and instantly had a sense that someone was shouting at my son. I went outside and I was right; it was Mrs. Rat shouting at Roy for playing with his ball in our back garden. It hadn't gone into her garden, but she could hear him playing with his ball and had decided that she had a right to shout at my son. In an instant I was up the top end of my garden and over the fence, right up to Mrs. Rat's front door to her house. I grabbed her by the throat and told her I had no idea what her problem was with my children and me but she had now overstepped the mark and no one spoke to my children like that without me reacting.

"What's your problem?" I asked Mrs. Rat.

"I don't have a problem," Mrs. Rat squirmed.

"Oh yes you have. We had no sooner moved into the property and you have done everything in your power to make yourself known to me! So you had better get your problem off your chest now!" I growled at her, still holding her by her throat.

"No, honestly," she whimpered.

"Well, let's me and you get something clear. Don't mess with my children or me. I don't take this sort of shit. Have you got that?"

I let go of her and climbed back over my fence. I shouted my eldest son out of the house. He had gone in thinking he was in trouble because he had upset the neighbour. I told him he hadn't done anything wrong and he had every right to play in his own garden.

About thirty minutes later a knock came to my front door. I answered it. Stood there were two uniformed police officers. I asked them what they wanted and I was informed that Mrs. Rat had made a complaint that I had assaulted her. I told the officers what had happened since we had moved into the property only some twenty-four hours earlier and the problems we had encountered with Mrs. Rat. The officer told me I shouldn't have grabbed her but that he would go back and see Mrs. Rat and tell her that they wouldn't be pressing charges against me and that if she had any problems that came from our address then she should contact the local council and complain to them. The officer asked me if I knew her. I told him I had never seen her before in my life.

***

Over the next few days a few people on the street said "Hello" as I had passed by them en route to either the shops or school. I noticed as the week passed that a man who regularly said "Hello" when he had been on his own totally ignored our presence when he was with his wife. I thought it funny how the wife never said "Hello" when we had passed on the street. I noticed this pattern with all female neighbours on the end of the street where we had moved in. I came to the conclusion this must have something to do with Mrs. Rat. One day, I thought, it will come out and I won't be going to the council to complain about Mrs. Rat, I would be at her door! I didn't have long to wait before the truth of whatever the problem had been would surface.

One Sunday afternoon while in my front garden mowing the two lawns the man who usually spoke when he saw me and my children had come up the hill and was making his way home. He stopped to say "Hello" to all four of us in the garden.

He had been speaking a few minutes when a female voice shouted. "Karl! Karl, get over here now!"

We all looked in the direction of her voice and saw the back end of her as she disappeared into a house and the door slammed shut. The man, who was obviously Karl, turned toward us and said he would have to go because his missus wouldn't be happy. I wanted to ask why but decided against it. I tried to convince myself that it was their problem, but my guts weren't holding that theory at all. That was it; my temper got the top side of me and I asked Rowan to mind my children. He said he would and I was over the road knocking on Karl's door!

"Is your wife in?" I asked as Karl opened the door.

He looked sheepish and said "Yes."

"Can you tell her I want to speak to her?" I insisted.

The woman appeared from behind the door. She was stood back from the door as we spoke.

"So what's your problem?" I asked her.

"I don't have a problem. I don't know what you are on about," the woman replied.

The door moved again and two more women stood there. They looked at me, I then proceeded to ask all three of them, "What is the problem?"

"I'll tell you what the problem is! Ever since we have moved onto this street we have nothing but attitude from everyone and I want to know why. I or my children don't know any of you. We haven't done anything to anyone, but the whole street seems to have a problem with us and I want to know why." I said.

The older of the two women who had come to the door spoke.

"Tell her! She has a right to know why."

Silence hung in the air; I was staring intensely at the wife. I could tell she felt awkward and didn't really want to speak to me.

"Well?" I asked.

She started to talk.

"Well, no one on this street wants anything to do with people that run around with firearms, and people who are always in trouble with the police. I don't want my children growing up in an area like that, and most of the mothers on this street feel the same."

"Firearms? What firearms? What are you talking about? I have never had anything to do with firearms in my life! Now what are you talking about?" I could feel my temper rising.

"Hey, don't take your problems out on her!" said the eldest woman.

"Problems? Do you want problems? Because I can soon cause them! You all talk bollocks! I've never heard such nonsense in my life! Firearms. Me? Don't think so!" I replied looking right into the elder woman's eye. The wife continued.

"Well, who in their right mind hides a firearm in a false wall inside the bathroom?"

"Bathroom? False wall? What are you talking about? Daft cow! You had better explain yourself because I'm slowly losing my patience!" I was growling and finding it hard to not lose my temper. It was definitely being tested to the max.

The wife continued to tell me that a few weeks before we had moved into the new house, late evening one Sunday a load of police cars and unmarked police cars had turned up outside our new home. The racket that was being made by the police when they had been inside our new home had drawn attention to the house, and everyone on the street had come out to see what the problem was. Mrs. Rat. had spoken to the police and they had told her.

She went on further, "Then there was the housing officer! Telling us that your family was dangerous and none of us should ever have anything to do with you!" She continued, "What with all the drug barons chasing you, how can you expect us to accept you on our street?"

"Stop right there. Let me get this straight. Not only have the police searched our home for firearms before we moved into it, but the housing officer told you that we were a dangerous family and that drug barons are chasing my family? Well, let me inform you that none of that bollocks that has come from your mouth is true. Do you hear me? I want the name of this housing officer. Now!" I was growling.

Just as I was finishing my sentence I heard a car door shut. The sound was coming from directly behind me. I turned round to see who it was—Mrs. Rat.

"Hi, Karl. Hi, Avaril. Is everything OK?" Mrs. Rat asked as she stood at her car door.

She was looking at all of us stood at the house door. Before I knew what I was doing I was over beside her grabbing her by her clothes.

"You bastards have caused me nothing but trouble since I moved here. Well I'm here to tell you it stops now!" I pushed her down over the bonnet of her car backward.

Karl was at the car by this stage. He was trying to loosen my grip against Mrs. Rat.

"Let go of her, missus. It isn't worth it. Let go! Let go!" He pleaded with me.

I let go of Mrs. Rat, who was in tears and obviously in shock at what I had done, but I now knew I had gotten my message home to her—don't mess with me! As she was getting herself together I turned around, hit her straight in the face, and said, "Don't ever cross my path again. Don't ever say I haven't warned you."

Karl tended to Mrs. Rat as I walked off toward my front garden, where Rowan and my children were. I was furious. How dare the police search my home? Admittedly we didn't live in the house at the time of the search, but it was still our house and we were paying rent on it. Also, what was the council's game? What where they talking about? Firearms! I knew that when the morning came I would be making two serious complaints: one to the police and the other to the council. I would be contacting my solicitor too. There was one thing the street now knew and that was that I wouldn't stand for any shit from them or anyone.

Over the course of time I actually befriended Karl and Avaril only to be let down by them at a later stage in my life. I discovered from the police that Karl and Avaril had been moved to their home by the police because Karl was a police informer and he had helped detain drug barons in the Bradford area.

Chapter Thirteen
Three New Children
Join the Household

It was autumn time of 1994. I had returned from a prison visit to Fred and was walking the road that led to my home. I looked toward my dining room window and I thought I saw a small child standing in it. I blinked to clear my eyes and to ensure I wasn't seeing things. No, I definitely wasn't seeing things. That was a young child standing at my window. But who the hell was he? When I left my home that morning, Rowan who lived with us was in the house but he had no children, so I was flummoxed as to whom this child belonged. A second later a woman I had never seen in my life stood beside the young child. She approached the window, looked at me walking up the road but didn't really acknowledge me, grabbed the small child from the window, and walked away. I had no idea who she was, but I was going to make it my business when I got in!

I entered my home and the woman was stood in front of the open fire holding the small child I had seen a few seconds earlier. The noise of other children crying filled the house. Who were these people? I walked into my front room, and there sat one of my brothers, Spring Heeled Jack. This woman I later discovered was his latest girlfriend. There was Rowan and two more small children. The house smelled terrible of human excrement.

"What is going off? This house smells! Open those windows!" I commanded. One thing I couldn't stand was smell of any sort.

My brother explained that he had no choice but to bring his new girlfriend and her children because she was fleeing her violent ex-partner.

He said, "I hope you don't mind, but I have no other option but for you to help me in this situation."

I didn't have a choice in the matter. There facing me were six hungry children, and three of those that needed their nappies changing. I never said anything—just got stuck into providing the nappies for the mother to tend to her children, while I started preparing a meal for all nine of us in the house.

The mother took her children one by one into the dining room to change their nappies. In turn each one was screaming in protest in having their nappies changed.

After tea my brother and the girlfriend went out for a walk with the children, saying they wouldn't be long before they were back. The phone rang; it was Fred. I told him what had greeted me when I had got home. He was sympathetic until I mentioned the girlfriend's name. He shouted "Get her out of that house!" But he wouldn't tell me why. I said until I knew why I wouldn't act on his instruction. My brother, his girlfriend, and the children came back from their walk and the mother immediately started putting the children into some sleepwear she had brought with her. Again she went into the dining room to get them ready and again the children were crying. When she had finished she came into the living room where we all were.

"They certainly don't like getting changed," I said.

She agreed, saying they were always like that. These boys were aged ten months, two years, and four years.

Later that night my brother left my home, saying he would be back in the morning to see us all and they would try and sort out some appropriate accommodation for them all to move to. He hadn't been gone an hour before the girlfriend asked where the local shop was and asked did I need anything bringing from it as she was going to get some cigarettes and would I mind just listening out for the children in her absence? I said we needed bread and gave her the money. I gave her directions and expected her back in ten minutes at the most.

She never returned. Me and Rowan sat up until the early hours of the morning, and she never phoned me to say where she was or when she would return. Rowan offered to sleep on the sofa and wait till she arrived back and then he would lock the house up. I agreed and went to bed.

***

The following morning I was awoken by the chorus of crying children. I got out of bed. Reggie, my youngest son was still fast asleep in my bed so I went downstairs to see what the problem was. When I got downstairs Rowan was already in the dining room trying to quieten these children. I entered the room and asked where the mother was. Rowan said she had not returned.

"Well, we best get these children up and fed," I said to Rowan. I knew it wouldn't be long before my two would be up so best get started while I had the opportunity. I instructed Rowan to go upstairs and run the bath while I stripped one child at a time so they could be bathed before they started the day. I did this with my own so there was no reason not to do this with these children. I started with the baby first.

I took him in the living room to remove his clothing so I could wrap him in a towel to take him upstairs to bathe him. I nearly died when I removed his nappy. This child was raw. There were blisters all over his genital area. He screamed when I removed the nappy. I shouted Rowan to come back downstairs and get me the baby bath and fill it with warm water. I thought it best to bathe this child while I held him in my arms. I anticipated he was going to cry when he was bathed, but there was no choice—he needed cleaning. He screamed. I wanted to cry for him. I had never seen anything like it. By this stage my own children were awake and downstairs, and Rowan was trying to occupy them and keep his eye on the other two children while I dealt with this baby. After I had finished with this baby I started with the two year old. When I stripped him he was the same—red raw and blisters all over his genital area.

"Poor children," I said allowed.

I had never seen anything like it. When I got to the third child I'd anticipated that he would be even harder to handle because he was stronger; he wasn't happy either when I removed the nappy he was wearing. He too was red raw and full of blisters in his genital area. Once I finished with these three children, I saw to my own children, and then it was breakfast time. The meal was like something out of the horror movies. These children didn't know how to eat with a spoon. Even the baby was refusing to eat. The eldest two were just screaming at the top of their voices and having a paddy like I'd never seen before. I just gave up trying to encourage them to eat. I abandoned breakfast time for these children. Once they realised I wasn't asking them to eat, they stopped screaming. I'd never seen anything like it before in my life. After breakfast I was sat having a smoke on the doorstep while the children were watching TV with Rowan. I sat thinking these children must have some sort of Urine infection, and if the mother was not back shortly I would have to contact my GP and get him to prescribe something for them. An hour passed and she still hadn't come back. Spring Heeled Jack had phoned and I had told him what I had found on the children. He said he would come straight away. I phoned to the GP's surgery and got an appointment for these children. We set off, all seven of us, down to the GP's surgery. Spring Heeled Jack had called just before we left and said he would be at my home address when I got back. When we finally got into see the doctor I explained what I had discovered and that the mother was missing. He asked did I know the name of the children. I could only say their first names; I didn't know their last name. When I had first been introduced to the mother her surname had been given to me but at this stage I had forgotten her name and for the life of me I couldn't remember. I advised the doctor that once my brother arrived I would get the information and call back to the surgery. The doctor examined the children one by one and then revealed his findings. He advised me that what I thought were blisters were in fact cigarette burns that had been deliberately administered. He gave me cream and directions on how to use it. He told me that I must find the name of these children and contact him as soon as I had the information.

**

When I got back to my home Spring Heeled Jack was waiting for our return. I advised him what had been said and he gave me the details the doctor required.

Within an hour Social Services was at my door. They asked how I had come to be in charge of these children; they also inspected my home and left saying they would be back in touch. They gave no time scale or released any information to me about these children. I was left just to cope with this situation. I discovered in those first twenty-four hours that the two children that were able to talk could only say their mother's name and the word no—nothing more. They had no understanding of the word yes and it was heart wrenching to think of what sort of life they must have been exposed to. Over the coming weeks the children started to trust me, my children, and Rowan. They learned for the first time how to actually play and eat with utensils, and eventually I managed to get these children into some sort of routine. A single bed and cot had been put into my room so that I had all of them in easy reach. It was hard work, but once they began to trust and start slowly acting like the children they were, it was amazing to see them smile. It was lovely to see them playing and not crying or fearing that they needed their nappy changing. They had started to live what I would call a normal life; they stopped trying to push us away and screaming. They stopped nipping us when we had close contact with them. They were learning how to show compassion by putting their arms around people and giving them love.

**

After two months these children had started saying our names. Social Services had long since been out of the picture so when they turned up one tea time with their mother I was shocked. I had so many questions I wanted answering, but there was no time. Social Services informed me that the children were leaving that day with their mother and them. I was given an address a couple of miles away from where I lived and informed that this would be where the children were to live with their mother. I had no say in the decision and the children screamed when they left my home. Somehow I felt they knew they were leaving all of us forever.

***

During this time I refused to go and see Fred in prison. There was no way I could manage all these children, the train, and visits to prison. Fred threatened every time he phoned that if I didn't go and see him soon he would start carrying out the threats he had made to me. But these children came before him or me. They were in need of help in more ways than I could give, but I was doing the best I could.

***

Just before Christmas of 1994 there was a knock at the front door one morning. A middle-aged man and woman presented identification to show they were from the Child Protection Unit and said they needed to speak to me. I asked immediately if this was in relation to the three young children that I had cared for.

They told me that the mother, father, and the children's uncle and aunt were all part of a paedophile ring. I was informed by these two officers that Fred had been aware of the mother, father, aunt, and uncle's behaviour because he was a known associate of theirs and that Fred had tried to secure conviction of them for the police, but there hadn't been enough evidence to arrest and charge the paedophile ring .

Chapter Fourteen
Attempted Murder

It was Christmas 1994, and time was coming around for the release of Fred from prison.

I had started to attend an adult education centre in the local area. While Fred was incarcerated I made contact with my mother. I begged her to not ask me anything. She told me I could tell her anything and that she would always be there for me and her grandchildren. My mother had become ill recently and she was staying with me and the children. My mother was under the care of the hospital and specialist for her illness. Christmas passed and just after the New Year Fred was released from prison.

***

During the first couple of weeks home Fred attempted to steal money from my mum, only to return the money when he was told if the money didn't reappear then the police would be called. Fred, being himself and true to form, tried to accuse the young lad who still resided with me and the children, but it was made perfectly clear—cough up or go down!

January passed with a lot of tension being aimed toward Fred's presence. No one in the house felt anything was safe. He had tried every-thing over the years and most of his tricks were known to me. I really didn't want him around, but as usual I had received the threats that Fred had over me for years.

February was a cold month and every spare penny was being paid toward bills to keep the house warm. Just like the previous month the atmosphere in the house was almost unbearable. Fred was still doing everything he could to steal anything he thought he could get money for or money itself.

***

"Help, help, Krisha," came a voice that disturbed my sleep.

I sat up in bed, listening in the black and stillness of silence in the house at night. Then I heard scuffling.

I heard my name being called from somewhere in the house.

I was out of bed in a shot and heading toward the stairs. I was sure it was coming from downstairs. As I hit the bottom step and turned on a small landing, there in the shadow, up against the wall, was a figure. I ran toward it because I could hear noises coming from the room my mother occupied. It sounded like my mother was gasping for breath. I recognised the figure of that of my eldest son. I ran into my mother's makeshift bedroom. I switched on the light.

My mother was grasping for breath. She was blue in the face, and her lips were even darker. I immediately went to my mother's aid.

"Mum! Mum! What's up? Mum, are you all right?"

"He tried to kill me! He tried to suffocate me!" My mother struggled to speak.

"What? What you on about Mum? Someone has tried to kill you?" I asked.

"Yes! Yes, he did!" my mother replied.

I turned to the direction of the hall where I had seen the shadow of my eldest son in the hallway.

"I haven't done anything! Honest mum! I haven't!" pleaded my eldest son.

I rose to my feet, my temper boiling. In an instant all sorts of thoughts were in my head at the same time I was making my way across the room to enter the hallway. What had my son done?

Out of the darkness and from the right of the doorway, out stepped Fred.

"Move out of my way! Move now," I ordered Fred as he stood between my son and me.

"It's not him! It's not your son! It's him." Grasping for her breath my mother managed to get this out.

I pushed with both hands at Fred's chest.

"What the fuck is happening? What have you done to my mother? What has my son got to do with this?" I was fuming.

I started moving toward Fred. Every possibility was running through my head. I knew from experience with him that there was nothing he wouldn't do. Fred's behaviour was always something to be concerned over, and I knew how determined he was when he got an idea in his head. But trying to murder my mother was another thing entirely! *I'm going to kill him!*

"He tried to suffocate me with my pillow!" My mother was finding it hard to breathe and was still gasping.

At the same time there was movement in the hallway. I heard footsteps coming downstairs and into the light came Rowan who lived with us. He had been awoken by the noise.

"You bastard! What have you done?" I launched toward Fred. He immediately withdrew toward the bedroom doorway.

"I've done nothing. I came down for a drink and heard a noise and I've just come to see what it's all about," Fred stated calmly.

"He's lying! He tried to suffocate me," my mother gasped.

"No, I haven't your delusional woman! I have not been anywhere near you," Fred said, walking toward my mother.

"Stop right there! You're going nowhere near her. Get yourself out of here. I'm calling the police." I growled at him in temper.

"You surely don't think I've done that?" he asked in a surprised voice.

My mother continued saying he had tried to suffocate her. We called an ambulance and the attendants listened to what my mother had to say. They said she must have been dreaming, and they left the property after checking my mother's vitals.

While everyone was in attendance I turned to Fred and my eldest son and said, "If you two were up to nothing, then why did it take for my mother to raise me from my sleep? Why did neither of you come to her aid when she was calling out? You were both down stairs when I got here. So come on, answer me! Why?"

They both stood there and said nothing. I expected some sort of pathetic excuse, but they both stayed mute. I glared hard at them both, and neither could look at me.

***

My mother was in hospital in a matter of days. She had given instructions that no one other than myself and Rowan who lived with us should be allowed to visit her. My mother asked the sister of the ward to put that on her records and to promise that her wishes were followed.

I then called one of my sisters to tell her our mother was in hospital. I knew that the message would be passed on to the rest of our family. My brothers and sisters attended the hospital, but our mother denied them access to her. My mum was only being visited by me and Rowan.

Suddenly my mother shouted out, "No! No! I don't want any of them in here. Get them out of here! I don't ever want to see them again!"

I turned to see members of my family walking up the ward toward my mother. I felt relieved that they had come, but my mum would not stop shouting. It wasn't long before the sister of the ward was on the scene and she asked them all to leave except for myself and the boy. "Mum, stop shouting! These are your children and they have a right to come and see you!" I said.

All the family was asking why they couldn't see their mother. The sister of the ward had to tell them it was her patient's request. I needed my family more than ever. But they didn't know it. I tried to get my mum to change her mind and let my brothers and sisters on the ward. She refused. And she meant it.

***

My mum died during an operation on 10 February 1995. Sat at home with the baby and Rowan, I had a sudden urge to phone the hospital; it was 12.25 pm. I needed to enquire after my mother and the operation. The ward telephone number was engaged. The house phone rang; it was the hospital asking if I could get to the hospital immediately.

"My mother's dead, isn't she?" I asked.

"No! The doctors just need to see you," the voice replied on the phone.

"Don't lie to me! I know my mother is dead—I can feel it! She is no longer with us. Please don't lie."

"No! Your mum is OK. Could you please get to the ward as quickly as possible?" the voice asked. Once at the hospital it was confirmed that my mum had passed away while on the operating table. The hospital asked me to identify my mother. I refused. There was no way I could do that. I instantly thought of Fred and Roy. There was no way I could leave the hospital until one of my sisters had got there and officially identified our mother. The doctors didn't want to end the meeting until identification had taken place. It was just a matter of time before one of them would get there.

It felt like the end of the world for me. My mother would never be there again for me to turn to. I blamed Fred and my eldest son for the death of my mother.

***

Once I had returned home I sat in silence after explaining to Rowan that my mother had died. I was waiting for Fred to come home, but he came home when he wanted. You couldn't set your clock by him, so it was just a case of waiting. I didn't know what I was waiting for, but I was waiting.

Finally Fred came home. I was stood outside my house speaking to one of the neighbours when he pulled up in a car.

"What's up?" Fred enquired as he came up the path. "You OK? What's wrong"? he continued. Obviously he could see that something was wrong.

Once inside the house I broke down in tears, explaining that my mother had died.

"So what you crying for? It's the best thing that could have happened to her! She would only have suffered more than she needed to," Fred said coldly.

That was it. I flew in temper at him. I just wanted to hit him so hard. Regardless of how much we fought in those few minutes Fred was not going to retract what he had just said to me.

The only thing going around in my head was "He fucking did it! I just know he did! He did this to my mother! His actions have led to this death!"

"Don't think I'm going to the funeral either, because I'm not!" Fred spoke in an adamant voice.

"No! You wouldn't dare would you? You're an evil bastard and we all know it." I had direct eye contact with Fred as I spoke.

He never again mentioned my mother, her death, or the upcoming funeral or asked how I was feeling. My son Roy never enquired over anything once he had been told my mother had died. He was thirteen years old and he had mastered how to be cold to emotion, and I couldn't understand his reaction.

Chapter Fifteen
Mr. Peacock

After the funeral it was a regular thing for there not to be any conversation between Fred and me. The days seemed to follow the same pattern. Fred would always be up first in the house at about 5:30am. Then Roy would get himself up and take himself off to school followed by me and Reggie. Most of the time the house was occupied by me and Reggie until Roy came home from school. Fred would pop back for about an hour around tea time, then he would be back out until whatever time he decided to come back home.

Fred had got himself a job. I never held my breath; I knew it would only be a matter of time before he would do something to ensure he didn't have to work. But with me instructing the Department for Work and Pensions that he along with Rowan had been stealing our benefit and we could not eat or look after ourselves because they was taking all the money and Fred had no regards for our welfare, the only way now for Fred to ensure he had some other income was to get a job. Whether that was legal or not, I didn't care. His benefit no longer had anything to do with me, and I didn't want to know how he would get by in life.

***

One morning I was in the kitchen at the sink. I heard a car door slam shut, like someone wasn't happy and was letting the world know about it. I looked up and could see an old man making his way up the path to my house. He came knocking at the door.

"Hello, is Fred in?" the man asked in a foreign accent.

"No. Can I ask who is asking?" I answered.

"Yes, you can. I'm Mr. Peacock. I'm his landlord. I haven't had rent from him in eight weeks and someone told me I would find him here."

"Landlord? He hasn't got a landlord!" I replied, shocked at what the man had said.

"Yes he has, and I'm it. That rent belongs to me, and I want it! You tell him that I will be back and I will not stop until I get my money or he is out." The man spoke with a growl in his tone.

"Hey, don't talk to me like that! Whatever you and him have going off is nothing to do with me. Whatever you're up to with him obviously is dodgy and nothing to do with me or my kids! Don't come to my home anymore!" I growled back and then slammed the door.

The man turned around and left the property. Landlord? What the hell was he talking about? I had refused point blank to feed Fred or do anything for him, but I knew nothing about him supposedly to be living somewhere other than where he was.

So now I had some idea of what he was up to. I could sense trouble would come again to my door from this man.

Chapter Sixteen
Mr. and Mrs. Spacker

One day I was in the house, like normal, and a knock came to the door. I answered it and found a bailiff from the courts stood on my doorstep. He asked me if I was who I was and then proceeded to read me my rights, saying I was under arrest for non-payment of fine. I explained that I had no idea what he was on about and that we would have to take Reggie with us if he was to arrest me and take me before the court immediately. The bailiff said that if I promised to attend the court before the end of the morning session and get someone to babysit my youngest son he would give me bail to appear in the court that morning. I agreed.

Later that morning I was at the magistrate's court and in the chamber at the back of the courtroom.

The magistrate asked me if I was aware of the outstanding fines that had been issued against me. I told them "No!", I had no idea. It unfolded that in the past eight weeks I had been issued at least twenty parking tickets that had all been issued on the same street but on different dates and times. I was asked was I the registered keeper of the vehicle, to which I confirmed. I explained to the magistrates that I had not been driving the vehicle since Fred had come out of prison and that he must have incurred the tickets. They asked me if I had received any notification through the post in relation to the matter. I answered, "No." The magistrates asked me to step outside while they discussed the matter.

While I sat outside the door, I fumed. I knew it was Fred because he had been the only one using the car. I gathered wherever this road was it would have a bookmakers on it; there would be no other explanation as to why he would keep parking the car where he knew he shouldn't. Then it hit me—I had been asked if I had been receiving notification about the outstanding fines. I knew I hadn't and when I got home I was going to make some enquiries as to whom I needed to speak to in relation to me not receiving any post at all. I hadn't had any post for weeks when I came to think about it and I was now convinced even more that Fred was up to something. If he had done something to the post that should have been delivered to our house, what was he trying to hide? Whatever it was he certainly didn't want me to know about it, but I now had been alerted and I would be damned if I wasn't going to find out! I went back into the room where the magistrates had been deciding what to do in relation to the information I had given them. They told me that the fines were a prisonable offence and that they did not hold me responsible for them after I had told them I had not been driving my car.

When I left the court I saw someone I knew. After talking about the morning's events in the magistrate's courts they informed me of the whereabouts of Fred—he was downtown at the County Court. Apparently there was some sort of trial on and he was sat listening to it.

I made my way to the County Court; he was going to get the length of my tongue no matter what. When I arrived I asked the usher how many trials were running that day and what courts. She explained to me that there was only one and she told me the number of the court it was being held in. I set off to the courtroom and stood outside where a large number of people gathered. I thought it must have been a very serious case. I entered the courtroom and there was Fred sat next to someone. He looked straight at the door as I opened it. I stood there staring back, then I left the court-room hoping he would follow me outside. He did. He wasn't happy that I was there, but I soon put him right that neither was I. During the course of the conversation Fred seemed obviously rather uncomfortable stood there speaking with me. It didn't take more than a few seconds to realise that he had a problem with a woman who stood over near the door to the court-house. I wouldn't even lower myself to ask. If this was a new woman, she was welcome to him. After having my say at Fred I left to make my way home to collect my youngest son from a friend's house where I had left him earlier in the day so I could attend court. I felt the woman's eyes on me and I nearly stormed over to her to ask her what the problem was. This was evident in my face because Fred gave me that glare, meaning I shouldn't bother or he and I would be falling out. I glared toward her with an acknowledging stare and left.

***

I arrived home and about ten minutes later Fred walked in the house. I knew there was something unusual about that; it was mid-afternoon and he was home. Instinct told me something was wrong, but there was no point in asking because I wouldn't be told the truth. My senses were heightened, and they had every right to be. It was only a matter of about thirty minutes and a knock came to the back door. Before I had chance to move Fred was on his feet making his way to the door. I heard him open the door and then the door close.

"Who was that?" I asked but got no reply. I asked again, and again I got no reply. This made me make my way to the kitchen, and as I approached I could see through the window the woman who had been at court. She and Fred were arguing. A man I had never seen before was now with this woman. He too was having some input. I stood staring at all three of them for a couple of moments and then thought, "I'm not having this outside my home." Before I realised it I was outside making my way toward all three of them. Fred's face dropped when he realised I was stood there. I instantly knew from the look on his face that something was seriously wrong.

"Who the fuck are you?" I asked, looking toward the woman and the man.

Fred tried to intervene, him telling me to get inside.

"Not a chance!" I growled at him, and he was taken aback by my response to his order.

The woman spoke first, and at some point her voice was echoed by the man who turned out to be her husband.

"Sorry, duck" she said and continued. "My name is Anna Spacker and this is my husband, Robert. I'm sorry we were staring at you earlier today when we were in the courthouse, but we want our money back!" she said.

The husband echoed, "Yes we do! We are sick of waiting for our money and the return we were promised."

I looked toward Fred. I could see he didn't want to be in this situation, so that gave me strength to continue with the conversation between Anna and Robert.

"Money? Return? What money and return? I don't know what you're talking about! Don't tell me you have given him money?" I said, indicating that I meant Fred.

"Yes," the couple answered together. The woman continued, "We have given him ten thousand pounds. We had to get a secure loan on our home because the profit involved was just too hard to resist," the woman said.

I stood glaring at Fred, who immediately answered the couple as to stop me from questioning him in the front of the couple. As he started to give them what I knew was a load of rubbish as an excuse I turned and walked back to my home and slammed the door as hard as I could, just to let all three of them who were outside know that I wasn't happy.

Again Fred had done something that had brought trouble to our door. I was catapulted back to our previous home and the terror we had faced there because of Fred. Yet again, strangers came to my door and trouble accompanied them. Twice in the space of a couple of days Fred had brought trouble to our door.

In a matter of minutes Fred was back in the house. He came to where I was and before I could say anything he said, "This is not what it looks like. I can explain!"

"Just do one! Get out of my home and get run over and die and make my day, you horrible bastard!" I spat at him.

He tried to talk to me, but I just didn't listen. I was back in the situation where a gun had been pointed at me and my baby and my senses were telling me there was going to be some serious trouble. Anything Fred had to say I just didn't want to know.

Within thirty minutes or so Fred had left the house; he knew no matter how much he tried to communicate with me he wasn't going to get anywhere, and he knew his exercise to convince me was going to be futile.

A few minutes after Fred had left a knock came to the back door of the house. I went to answer the door and stood there was Anna and Robert. I instantly thought, "Here it comes." But instead they asked if they could come in and speak to me because they had realised that I knew nothing about what was going on between them and Fred and they obviously wanted to inform me. The truth unfolded and I was surprised that what appeared to be two very educated people had so easily fallen for some fraudster's lies and had accepted the word of a total stranger.

Anna Spacker was the dominant one in the marriage—that was easy to see. She made all the important decisions; I could tell by the way she conducted herself and her husband just went along with whatever she said. They had met and befriended Fred only a few weeks earlier, and he had told them of a betting scam that both he and I had pulled off some years ago. Fred and I came across a scam whereby we placed bets after the horse races had run and we had been paid out by the bookmakers. He had taken them to the races and performed the scam with his own money, and they had seen the return and results. This had happened over a few weeks. They said they felt they could trust him to go to the races with their money and they told me they had received some return, but after a week or so Fred had stopped going to visit them and they had not received a penny of any return or their own money. I sat and listened, and I could tell they were telling the truth. I was thinking to myself, *Idiots! How could anyone trust a stranger with their money like that? I wouldn't even do that with my own family, let alone a stranger.*

It became clear that these two individuals were stupid and had opted for what they thought was a win–win situation. I suppose in a way they had got what they had deserved. But what I knew was this had nothing to do with me or my children, and I told them so. I told them that I felt sorry for what had happened to them and if I was them I would go to the police, but I had to insist that they never come to my door ever again. This had nothing to do with us and they had to understand that. I asked how they had ended up at my door in the first place. The couple went onto tell me that they had only known Fred's address near the town centre. He had rented a bedsit. They never knew he had a child with anyone or that we even existed until that very day, when they had got so fed up with waiting for Fred to go to their home with either their money or some sort of explanation that they decided to visit what they knew was his home address. That day the landlord of the property had been there and he had told them where I lived and advised they try my address. En route to my address they had spotted Fred outside the County Court, so they parked and went to confront him. By the time they had parked and got to the courthouse Fred was inside one of the courtrooms, so they were waiting for a chance to speak to him. They never got that chance because they went to their car to put a ticket on it again and when they had returned Fred was no longer present in the courthouse. That is why they came to my home address. The couple left my home knowing I didn't want them anywhere near me or my children, and I left them with no doubt I would go to the police and report Fred. What they did from then on was their decision.

***

I never saw Mr. and Mrs. Spacker at my home again, but weeks later our paths crossed again. That meeting wasn't planned by either them or me. Fred had just stopped the car, saying he had to see someone. He disappeared down a drive and moments later Mrs. Spacker had come up the drive and insisted that I come in her house. Once I was in the house, which was a converted church, I realised why Fred had targeted them. The house shouted *money!* And Fred had not been slow to feed from their wealth.

It was becoming clearer by the day that Fred was bang at his criminal activities, and prison had not deterred him from such acts. He was never going to stop getting in trouble and whenever I tried to leave or say he must stay away from me and the kids he always reminded me that he had control over me and at any given time he could have me arrested and I would never see my children ever again and they would never want to know their mother if she had been in prison even after her release. Fred continuously reminded me that he worked for and on behalf of the police and anything I had to say would never be believed by the police because they hated me and my family. My life with Fred since the armed aggravated burglary at our previous home had shown me that the police didn't like me or my family and at any time I had been in any sort of contact with the police they had made it perfectly clear that they knew I was Fred's wife and Spring Heeled Jack's sister and our relationship was one that was being watched by every police officer in the country.

Fred was still working and said that the job was going well and was interesting; he was enjoying the role he played. He was a salesman selling dry, frozen meat and such, and he said his job took him all over the country. I always had my doubts about anything he had to say, but at least I had my benefits to feed my children and to run my home the best I could. I didn't rely on Fred for anything. He would sometimes come home with gifts for the children. To them he was a saint because he could give them presents and treats, something I wasn't able to do. I knew he did this to undermine me and put me in the bad light of not being able to give the treats they wanted. I couldn't explain to the children how life was living on benefits and neither could I have expected them to understand.

Chapter Seventeen
Mr. and Mrs. Church

Fred was in the house one evening about seven o'clock, which was unusual for him. He had ordered that no one in the house should pick up the phone if it should ring. I had questioned why we shouldn't, and he said, "Because I said so and I mean it!"

The phone was ringing on and off for about an hour and I was getting fed up hearing it. I was going on at Fred asking why, and eventually he left, reminding us that we must not answer the phone.

Fed up and in desperation to stop the ringing I picked up the phone.

"Oh hello, is that Fred?" said a man.

"No! Can I ask who is calling?" I replied.

"Is that Fred's wife?" the man questioned.

"No, I'm not his wife. Can I ask who is calling?"

"Oh, hello my name is Mr. Church and Fred gave me this number to call if I ever needed to contact him for any reason. He told me if he wasn't in, then his wife would take the call and get a message to him. Have I got the right number?" the man asked.

"Fred is not married to me and I have never heard him mention you. What message would you want me to pass to him when I see him next?" I answered.

"Yes, I and my wife are a bit concerned that we haven't seen him for over a week and we need to see the books for the business we have invested in. So if you could just ask him to give us a ring as soon as possible," the man said.

"Business? What business? I don't know what you're talking about," I answered.

"Well, if you could just pass on the message, then he will know what you're talking about I'm sure!" the man replied.

The conversation ended and I put the phone down. I was on high alert again. Fred was up to something and I had no clue what it was. Why he had given my house telephone number out to someone? Why was Fred trying to avoid that call? What I knew was I was going to find out when he next came home.

I got the usual explanation from him—that he hadn't got a clue who the man was or anything about any business and he would have no trouble speaking to whomever it was who had called. He tried to reassure me he wasn't up to anything and no trouble would be coming to the door. *We will see!*

***

A few days passed and Mr. Church kept calling and asking if Fred was in or had I passed on the message. I answered him honestly, saying that Fred had repeated he did not know who the man was and that he had no business with anyone. The man was becoming upset on the phone and told me to pass the message on to Fred that if he didn't go to see him and his wife within twenty-four hours they would be going to the police. I informed the man not to wait if he felt that something was wrong with whatever they were involved with, especially if it involved Fred. I assured him I would definitely tell Fred when I next saw him.

Later that afternoon when Fred came in I passed on the message. He didn't seem alarmed. Shortly after, he left the house, not saying where he was going. He arrived back about eight that night with a bundle of papers in his hand. I asked what they were, expecting him to not tell me, but he shocked me. He sat down and told me that he had been to Mr. and Mrs. Church's home and he had taken a contract that all three of them had signed in relation to a business venture that did not exist. He revelled in the fact that he had fraudulently taken thousands of pounds from an old couple and ripped them off. He finished by saying "They are loaded—they won't miss it, and what can they now take to the police?"

Chapter Eighteen
Mr. Pillock and Miss Chips

Tina, a friend of mine from since time began, was getting married. I had heard about her engagement but I hadn't seen Tina in a long while. When I heard the news, I wished her all the happiness one friend would give to another. The only thing was I hadn't seen Tina for a few years by this stage so I couldn't wish her happiness to her face.

One Sunday afternoon as I sat playing indoors with my kids a knock came to the door. I went to answer it and stood there was Tina and a man, whom I presumed was the man she was going to marry.

"Hello, stranger! Longtime, no see! How you doing?" I asked her.

"Fine. Just thought I'd call and see if you are OK," she replied.

"How did you know where I lived?" I asked, realising I hadn't seen her since I last lived in Sheffield.

"Oh, I made some enquiries and I was given your address," she replied.

I asked them both in and made a cuppa. We had a quick catch up about what had happened in her life since I last saw her, then I realised something was wrong. I could sense it. The man who was to be her husband, Adam, had not said one word since I had opened the door and he wasn't even trying to engage in any sort of conversation. I felt awkward in his company but I didn't know why. After a short while I made some excuse, saying I had to be somewhere shortly and that it had been nice to see her and she should call again. As she was leaving she asked where Fred was. At that time I didn't think anything wrong with that question because she knew him. I said I didn't know and I didn't care if I was being honest. The man looked at me with a questioning sort of look on his face. I immediately thought that there was something strange about this man. They then left; I wished she would have come to see me on her own because her man gave me the willies. If she phoned before she came next time as promised I was going to ask her to come on her own. Later on in the day, when Fred came in and during general chit chat with Roy, Fred discovered that Tina had been by. He proceeded to question me about the visit.

"What's it got to do with you? And why are you asking?" I snapped at Fred.

"No reason. It's just that I haven't seen her in years and was just asking how she was," Fred replied.

I thought fair enough answer and left it there, not deliberating about the visit with him.

***

The following day a knock came at the door. I answered and to my surprise Tina and Adam were stood there again.

"Hey up. Twice in a week. Can't keep you two away," I commented.

Adam only said "Is Fred in?"

He took me by surprise. It was the way he said it and the tone in his voice. I could tell that he definitely knew Fred. I looked at Tina, and her head went down to the floor. Something was wrong, but what?

"Tina, what's up?" I asked staring at her and ignoring Adam.

She didn't get the chance to answer before he said, "Well, is he?"

"Excuse me, but do I know you? I don't answer to people I don't know," I barked at him.

"Is he in?" Tina asked me.

"Why?" I replied.

Silence fell among all three of us.

I spoke.

"Tina what's up?"

Adam spoke.

"Do you know we get married in the morning?"

I stood looking at him, thinking "What a funny thing to ask me. Why was he asking me if I knew that?" I had told them on their previous visit that I would have loved to go to their wedding, but my life didn't allow such pleasures. I was just about to ask him why he had said that when Tina said they had better come in. I stood to the side of the door to let them in, and I never took my eyes from the man accompanying Tina. He gave me bad vibes. My instinct kicked in and rather than wait for them to speak I did.

"You had better tell me what's wrong. I can tell there is something wrong, so, Tina, I demand that you tell me now!"

83

"We're sorry for coming again to your house but we are left with no choice—things are desperate!" she continued. "Fred was supposed to come to our house last Saturday and bring the menus for us to give to our guest. He said they could have a choice of four menus." She went on, "Well, me and Adam have tried paging him and he isn't responding to them. Things are now at crisis point and in a few hours we have all these guests coming and we don't know what they are going to eat!" she explained.

I was dumbstruck. What was she on about? How could Fred cater a wedding? Where was all this food coming from? And why hadn't anyone informed me of what had been arranged?

"You what? You're telling me something I know nothing about." I looked straight at the man. "And don't you ever come to my home and speak to me like you just have done ever again!" I was making myself perfectly clear to this man that I didn't like him.

"You say that you have been in contact with Fred and neither you nor Fred have told me! How long has this plan been discussed between you all? And you come here to my home asking his whereabouts? Answer me, Tina! I need an explanation now!" I snapped at both of them. It unfolded that Tina and Adam had given Fred three and half thousand pounds to deliver the catering for their wedding and he had asked Tina not to inform me of their business arrangement because he wanted to surprise the children and me with a holiday with the money he would make. That had been the reason Tina had withheld the information from me when she had visited the day before. Now the situation had become critical because Fred had contacted them, the night before their previous visit to me, saying he would be around to see them and there was plenty of time to organise everything. He had assured them they had nothing to worry about. Now was the eve of their wedding and still he hadn't been to see them. I couldn't believe what Tina was telling me. For a moment I felt pity for her and her husband to be, and then the anger kicked in.

"You come here telling me that you kept important information like you have from me and what? What do you expect from me now? I can assure you I knew nothing about what you have just explained but what I am sure of is that there will be no holiday for the children and me and I can categorically tell you from my experience with Fred that you will not be getting any catering from him. My advice to you both is go to the police and report what he has done. If he comes up trumps for you, then I will be shocked. He must have arranged for the catering to be done elsewhere because as you can see it's not taking place here!" I growled at them both.

Adam spoke, "So what do we do now?"

I replied, "I have no idea, but you can see for yourselves the catering is not taking place here, so do as I tell you—go to the police."

Turning to Tina I said, "You call yourself a friend? I don't think so! How could you let someone like Fred put a division of loyalty between us? You have even let yourself down and all your guests, it now appears. Don't even think about putting any of the blame on me for the situation you two find yourselves in. Now I'm telling you to leave my home!"

Chapter Nineteen
The Numerous Victims
of Fred's Crime Sprees

During this same period I was met many times when answering my own door to hammers, machetes, and threats of violence from total strangers all telling me the same thing—that they wanted their monies back for cars that Fred had purchased from them using fraudulent cheques he had made or that they had been told by the police that had been dealing with their reported crime that the person responsible for their loss lived at my home. I have been held by the throat, pinned against my back door while receiving death threats if I didn't tell them where Fred was. All visitors said they would return until they found him.

Each time this happened I would immediately phone the police, and they would, of course, deny any involvement with telling the whereabouts of the person they believed to be responsible for the reported crimes.

I was asked every time by the police, "Why have you phoned us? You know people in the underworld who could deal with this and there is no way you were afraid of the people that have turned up at your door. You're wasting our time and you shouldn't commit the crime if you don't want these people at your door."

Why did I bother? They had it in their heads that I had something to do with whatever had happened and I had no doubt that Fred had put those ideas in their heads. I was trapped all ways around. I had two children to protect and no one willing to help me. I was so alone and no one even cared. I had no family to turn to, no friends, and not even the authorities that were supposed to be there to protect everyone. I promised myself that if anyone ever hurt my children I would kill them at whatever the cost. They were innocent just like me, and no one cared for our safety. Fred didn't seem to be bothered when I argued about the people turning up at my door with weapons and threats. His attitude was "Just deal with it!" I really felt like I was losing my mind. I hated going out of the house for fear of being attacked by total strangers at any given time. I had no control over anything.

Chapter Twenty
The Funeral Director

I was sitting at home when the phone rings. I pick it up. "Hello. It's your money, so you speak first," I said.

"It's me, young'un." It was my sister, Ellen. "When are you going to pay the funeral director? He has been on to us and he needs payment as soon as possible"

I explained that as far as I knew the Department of Social Security should have sent the money direct to the funeral director who had dealt with my mother's funeral arrangements. I explained that I would contact them and try to get a time scale and would call her back.

***

No one in the family had money to bury my mother, and that had resulted in me approaching the Department of Social Security for the help that we needed to bury our mother. They had given instruction as to how much they would contribute to the funeral, and if the cost was higher than the amount they had stated then we would have to find the money ourselves.

I contacted the Department of Social Security by telephone. It transpired that they had sent a cheque addressed to me and in my name to my home address some weeks before. I explained I hadn't received it and that the funeral directors were asking for payment. The personnel officer said he would check their system to see where the cheque had been cashed and get back in touch that day. When he called back, he informed me that the policy at that time for anyone making a claim for funeral expenses would have received a cheque in their name for them to cash so they could pay the funeral directors instead of letting funeral directors be aware that families were paying the funeral cost via the Department of Social Security. The officer asked if I would go to their office immediately so this situation could be sorted. I agreed. I got my children ready and I walked into town. Once at the office I was taken into an interview room and the two officers present showed me a cheque made out in my name for the amount of the cost of the funeral; it had been cashed at a place where people can take cheques to get cashed straightaway for a fee. I was asked to make a statement to the effect that I had not received the said cheque and that I had not given anyone permission to cash the cheque on my behalf. The department said that they would issue another cheque to me for the cost of the funeral and that the said cheque would be given to the police to investigate. I told them I had no problem with the police but asked the Department to send the cheque straight to the funeral director under the circumstances. They agreed.

I contacted my sister later in the day and explained the cheque should be with the funeral director within two days.

When Fred came home later that day I didn't ask him if he knew anything about this cheque. I told him I knew somehow he was responsible for this cashed cheque and I hoped he would get caught and sentenced for his evil ways.

Chapter Twenty-One
My Departure

After the death of my mother I couldn't stand to be near Fred, and once Spring Heeled Jack was released from his long-term prison sentence, he had come to live at our house, so I was sure I was now going to get away from Fred. Rumour had it that Spring Heeled Jack had been stitched up by the police for burglaries he hadn't committed and had been sentenced by the courts and he had served roughly 8 years before being released. Even though my brother, Spring Heeled Jack, knew nothing of what my mother had alleged before her death regarding Fred trying to kill her, I felt that having him in my home was giving me the strength I needed to get away from Fred. Unfortunately, after a few months of living at my home Spring Heeled Jack moved out to live with his new girlfriend. After revelations from Rowan about Fred's continued criminal pursuits, I decided enough was enough regardless of what would happen to me. After going to the police and reporting the disturbing details I had been given about the rape of a disabled woman and I had been told by Rowan that Fred did this. I believed he was capable of the said crime. But I was getting nowhere with them, I was at the eve of my departure from my home.

***

In the early hours of the morning an argument broke out between Fred and me. During the course of the argument Fred admitted to me that he had attempted to murder my mother. Fred also revealed that being with me was a bonus to the police he worked for. Fred went onto state that he had been planted in the same cell at prison as one of my other brothers, Napolean with a view to obtain information about Spring Heeled Jack. Apparently he had been posing problems to the police involved in the handling of his case. Fred continued making statements during the course of the argument. He stated that by the end of that month, Spring Heeled Jack would be back in prison because Fred had been working with the police to ensure this would happen. He even stated what, where, and why Spring Heeled Jack was going to be arrested and charged. Fred really thought he had the upper hand, and he enjoyed every minute of the impact his words were having on me. He got pleasure from it; I could see it in his face. He meant every word. I couldn't wait for morning to arrive so I could take the children away from this evil monster. I was determined to do it at whatever cost.

When I woke the next morning Fred was already downstairs with our youngest son; the eldest Roy had already left for school. I left the house in my nightwear and I took the baby with me, stating I would be back later in the day to get my eldest son Roy, once he returned from school.

***

Upon my return to the house later that day Spring Heeled Jack and I were met with a wall of police officers who refused me entry to the property and stated that if I wanted custody of my son Roy then I should go to court for him because he has said he wanted to live with Fred. I was furious at the police and I told them so. I couldn't understand how they had the power to stop me going into my own home and removing my son. I was met with aggression from the police. An inspector had been called to the scene; that's how serious the confrontation had become. The police, with their death ray glare and threats of being arrested and trying to pervert the course of justice, led to my brother talking me into walking away and leaving my eldest son Roy until I had seen a solicitor.

***

Within a week the court date had been set; it was due to be heard in the Chesterfield area because that is where my eldest son was residing at the time of the application.

***

On the morning of the court hearing I left the South Yorkshire area heading for Chesterfield with Spring Heeled Jack. En route to the court we stopped at a supermarket in the Chesterfield area, local to the courts. We purchased goods and petrol before heading off to the court for the hearing. Once we arrived at the court we found the solicitor who was representing me, and all three of us went into a side room only to be joined moments later by Roy's father and his wife. An usher came into the room moments later and looked straight at me; he then asked if he could have a word outside with the solicitor. I thought nothing unusual about that. While the solicitor was away with the usher someone in the room drew my attention to the window and what was happening outside on the downward-sloping bankings that approached the courthouse. I saw armed police officers and police dog handlers, all in full riot gear. All four occupants in the room were guessing that there must be someone very dangerous in the courthouse or someone had escaped to call for that sort of turn out from the police." The door opened and the acting solicitor asked my ex-husband if he could have a word with him and his wife outside. I looked on puzzled. Why would my solicitor want to talk to my ex-husband and wife, and why not in front of me? In a matter of milliseconds I understood why. The door flung open and there were screams of "Get on the floor! Get on the floor! Now!" The commands were deafening. Before Spring Heeled Jack and I knew it, we had guns pointed at us and up at us. Spring Heeled Jack was immediately tackled to the floor and ambushed; at the same time I was receiving the same treatment.

"Bastards!" I shouted at them.

Both Spring Heeled Jack and I fought back. We had no idea what was happening; it could have been anything. In the doorway, officers who first came through the door were plain clothed, followed by uniform.

"Where's the fucking gun, you bastard?" asked the police.

Gun? Gun? What fucking gun? What are they on about?

The deafening shouting continued. Before I knew it I was handcuffed both on my feet and hands; someone was knelt on top of me and I was face down.

"So where's the fucking gun, you bastard?" Someone growled in my ear. I could feel the warmth of their breath on my face.

I remained silent; there was no way on this Earth I was going to answer to anyone, not after the way I had just been ambushed.

"Where's that fucking gun? Tell us now. Think you can play on our patch? Eh?" Someone again was shouting at the side of my face.

I heard and saw shoes. Laying there I said nothing. A pair of shoes became visible right in front of my face. A new voice. Ginger, he was a policeman that I came to know over the next few hours.

"Where's the gun? Tell us because if you think we will not find it, you're wrong! The longer this goes on the more trouble you're in. Now tell us where that gun is!"

I still refused to say anything. How could these people treat me this way? And what were they talking about? I'd never held a gun or used one. *Fred—whatever this is about it as something to do with him.* I was thrown into a chair. Thud!

"You will tell us because we will find the gun! Tell us," a plain clothes officer shouted in my face.

No way would I speak to someone who was treating me this way. I remained quiet, thinking, "Until someone explains to me what this is all about, you can do whatever you want, but I'm saying nothing."

On top of that I knew I was in the police jurisdiction where Fred was a registered informer. Blondie and Silver worked this area in what I had now learnt was the serious crime squad. For hours I was being asked the same thing over again by the police. Ginger appeared on and off throughout the next four or five hours, still wanting to know where the gun was. Finally Ginger asked me where I had been that morning before I had arrived at court.

"Why?" I asked.

"You know why! You and Spring Heeled Jack have been to your last address before you attended here and you have threatened Fred. You did this by putting a shot gun down his throat and threatening that if he comes to court today you will be back to sort him out if you don't get custody of your son!" growled Ginger.

"Bollocks!" I growled back.

"You think you're big don't you? Playing in the big league now! Don't you? Well, let me assure you you're going down for this! You don't mess on our patch." Ginger spat his words through clenched teeth.

"How's about bollocks! I suppose I've robbed the fucking crown jewels as well! And Fred, well say no fucking more! I should have known he would be behind this and you twats go full out because he accuses me! How's about do one! And send me to prison? Well if that's how you fuckers operate then get fucking on with it!" I growled back.

"You think you're a hard fucking nut, don't you? Well I've news for you both, you and your brother. You will get six years if not more if we have anything to do with it. And you think we will not find the gun? Well just watch!" Ginger grew even angrier.

All sorts of thoughts were running through my head. Fred had used a gun in his allegation; he was using his life experiences to ensure he got maximum impact from the police. I knew how his mind worked. I knew my brother and I had done nothing wrong and I knew the police would not believe a word we had to say against their registered police informer. There was no point trying to say anything so I still remained silent. Ginger kicked his chair back and left the room with some officers, while others stayed in attendance with me in the room. I was fuming—how dare these officers treat me this fucking way? How dare they? Fred! Well, I knew that I had expected trouble for myself, but including my brother was unbelievable and unforgiveable. Fred was going all out to ensure he caused me as much pain as he could. The trouble was I didn't know what to expect next from him.

During the course of the afternoon while I still sat handcuffed, hands and feet, I played over and over the threats Fred had promised to execute if I ever left him. Now he had started his plan. Trouble was I would be blind to anything he did, but I felt he would definitely follow this course of action and whatever was going to come in the future would be a rerun of his life experiences.

Ginger came back; he had changed his approach to me. "Just tell us where your car is and the gun. You are not doing yourself any good. Just answer our questions, and we can get this cleared up."

"Bollocks," I blurted back at him. "Cleared up? Cleared fucking up? How dare you? Who do you think you are? Oh, that's right—the police! The police who protects Grasses! You involve innocent people in things they don't consent to! That's who you are! Bollocks," I shouted back at Ginger.

Ginger was on his feet in a flash and bent right into my face.

"Listen here. What Fred does has nothing to do with this. You have a gun and you think you can run around our patch threatening people. Don't think so! Why do scum like you do these sort of things? Believing we are not going to react is beyond me," he said. "Just tell us where your car is. That's all we are asking at this moment. Don't think you and your brother will escape us because you can't. Just tell us!" he growled.

I snapped.

"Listen here, you. I'm not scum! Neither my brother nor I have done anything wrong. And before you say they all say that I'm telling you the truth." I looked him in the eye.

"Well, tell me your whereabouts before you came to court," he said.

"I'll fucking tell you—I went to a local supermarket. I did some shopping for my brother's wardrobe and got some petrol. If you don't believe me go and watch it on their camera," I hissed at him.

"Which supermarket?" he asked.

I gave the officer the details and also the details of where my car was parked.

Ginger and some officers left the room, saying they would be back. In the mean time I was left still under armed guard, handcuffed, with no food or drink.

"Bastards," I hissed in the direction of the officers who were guarding me. They just laughed. Ginger arrived back a few hours later. He told me he had found and searched my car and he could not find a gun.

"I will tell you again, I've never had a gun. He's telling you bollocks! Not that you believe a word I say so I don't know why I'm bothering. He's taking the piss and maybe you will realise that soon," I said to the officer.

Ginger left the room again and a few hours went by without an incident. Eventually Ginger popped his head around the door and said to the guarding officers, "Come on and bring her!"

I was pulled to my feet by the officer and escorted to the courtroom. I was still cuffed, with armed police officers in front of me and behind me and police dog handlers.

I passed Ginger.

"Where's my brother?" I asked as I was being pulled along by the officers.

Ginger replied, "Don't you mind. He will be going back to where he has recently come from." He had a smirk on his face.

"Your both as guilty as hell and we will find that gun!" he replied all cocksure. Entering court two I saw nothing but police officers standing all around the edges of the courtroom. Some were armed. *What the hell?* I was guided down to the front of the courtroom to where my solicitor sat. On arrival at the front seating area, my solicitor glanced at me momentarily.

"Hello," a quick eye contact moment came from the solicitor.

The court already had a magistrate present when I had entered the courtroom. My solicitor stood up to speak on my behalf and was stopped short in his tracks by the magistrate.

The magistrate spoke.

"Application denied on behalf of the mother. We will not tolerate such behaviour and this case will now be passed to the county court. It is far too serious to be dealt with by this court. The child of the family will remain where he is residing at the moment."

My solicitor tried to object and was immediately shot down by the magistrate.

"Case dismissed. Remove her from this court, "the magistrate ordered.

Fred was sat on the opposite seating at the front of the court. I looked across at him. He had a smug glint in his eye.

"You bastard!" I yelled in his direction. "You have done and made something up, you grassing bastard."

Thud! I was hit in the back and within seconds I was being dragged out of the courtroom.

"You're a lying bastard and one day these twats will see you for what you are!" I yelled.

Thud! I was hit in the back again. This time it knocked me off my feet.

"Bet you're laughing your head off, aren't you? You're playing them just right, you bastard!" I was shouting as I was being half-dragged across the staircase landing and before I was dragged down the courthouse steps into a waiting police van with blacked-out windows. It had been reversed up to the courthouse entrance. Dogs were snapping at my face all the way down the stairs and until I was thrown in the van.

***

At the police station I was placed before the custody sergeant and then put, still handcuffed, into a room. About half an hour passed and the door opened to the room. An inspector walked in with a police officer; immediately I became abusive.

"OK bastard, come to have a look? Have Blondie and fucking Silver sent you? He's playing you and you're letting him!" I growled at the two officers.

"Shut up and listen to what I have to say," said the inspector.

"No, you listen to me! I have been accosted by the police and accused of something I have no knowledge of, dragged around, hit in the back, been made out to be something I'm not, and I want these fucking cuffs off now," I screamed at the inspector.

They stood there just staring at me; finally the inspector spoke. He turned to the officer and ordered that the handcuffs be removed. He asked me how long I had been in handcuffs. I was uncooperative, I hated the two men stood in front of me; they were a part of a bigger picture and I knew that I would not get anywhere with them. One of the officers left the room and returned with some keys. He unlocked and released the cuffs.

"Calm down. You're not doing yourself any good behaving like this. We need to sort this out and as quickly as possible," said the inspector.

I was shouting all sorts of things at the inspector, from abuse to unlawful detention and wrongful arrest. The inspector stood there looking at me. Getting nowhere with me fast, the inspector turned around and left the room with the officer.

"Bastards," I hissed. Where was my brother? The words Fred had said to me were rolling around in my head along with thoughts of the police and their treatment of me, my children, the magistrate, the whole situation. I knew neither my brother nor I had done anything and I knew Fred was playing the scene to the max. The inspector and the officer came back in the room.

"Right, I have listened to everything you have said and I can assure you I will be dealing with the officers concerned after I've spoken with you," explained the inspector. A short while later, just as the inspector had promised, two officers entered the room and started to question me about my brother and my whereabouts and actions of the day. I explained, as I had done earlier in the day.

"We have witnesses that you were at the house with a gun, along with your brother," said an officer.

Immediately I started shouting.

"Bollocks! This is a stitch up and we all know it. Fuck you and your fucking witnesses! We have not been to my house. You are fucking stitching us up and we both know it," I said, looking the investigating officer right in the eye.

"We will be remanding you in custody until we sort out the matter," said the officer.

"I tell you what, twat—do it! Go on if that makes you feel that you have power. Oh you must protect that grass. Fred! Then go ahead and fucking do it." I spat my words at the officer. "I and my kids mean fuck all to you! Your duty is to protect the Grass. He is fucking playing you, I'm telling you!" I hissed. I went on to shout at the officers. "Fuck you!"

***

Later that night around midnight I was bailed from police custody until four weeks later. I questioned the police as to where my brother was. They told me to go home and forget him because he was going back to prison; there was no way he was being released. I refused to leave the police foyer. The police threatened to re-arrest me if I didn't leave, but I stood my ground and wouldn't leave the building.

"I want to see my brother before I go anywhere," I insisted.

The police said I couldn't, but I insisted. A door opened and out walked my brother; he too had been let out on bail.

"Bastards!" I snarled at the officers. They just laughed at me. They had obviously wanted to cause my brother difficulty in getting home that night. We were both miles away from his home address. When Spring Heeled Jack and I reached the car where I had parked it, we were in for an unexpected surprise. In their search of the vehicle the police had dismantled the dashboard, which meant we could not drive the car.

***

We returned to my brother's home via tow truck. As we reached the road to my brother's home, out of nowhere in the dead of night a light shone directly on the emergency vehicle from above. The police helicopter had obviously been following us since we had left the Chesterfield area and wanted to let the occupants of the vehicle know they were there.

As we pulled up outside my brother's home, the helicopter still hovered about, so everyone on the street came to windows in their homes. The noise was tremendous from the helicopter. Suddenly my brother's girlfriend appeared on their drive.

I stood there in the light that shone on us from above and hurled abuse toward the helicopter. Once I got on the drive I noticed that my brother's car had no wheels on.

"What has happened to your car?" I asked.

"Wait till you get inside. I have so much to tell you!" says his girlfriend. "Armed police have been here all day, and so has the helicopter on and off. They ripped my home to pieces and they wouldn't tell me anything. When I asked where you both were they wouldn't tell me anything. They just kept asking if I had seen either of you with a gun."

Inside the house the story unfolded that the police had taken electrical equipment apart and left it in pieces. They had dismantled furniture and left it that way. My brother's car had received the same treatment as mine, even though it was parked on his drive. They had even taken off the covers for plugs and light switches. The police had done this in front of four small children. They had shown no mercy.

***

The following day I complained to my solicitor only to be told, "What do you expect?" That was the end of my relationship with that firm of solicitors who were representing me. Everything was eventually put back together at no cost to the police.

Chapter Twenty-Two
The Journey to the Border

We started out from the South Yorkshire area en route to Chesterfield for the court hearing. It was the first appearance before the courts after the allegations Fred had made, and he'd gotten maximum impact from the police. Spring Heeled Jack and I were still on bail, but both of us were adamant that we would be attending the court hearing. I had left my youngest son, Reggie, in the care of Spring Heeled Jack's girlfriend again.

"That helicopter keeps circling us!" Spring Heeled Jack noticed this after we had been on our journey for a few minutes. We continued on our journey, Chesterfield bound.

"I'm telling you, that helicopter is following us," he stated again after we had been travelling a few miles further.

"Get ready then because he will have done something else, no doubt in my mind!" I replied.

I was now sure we were being followed by the police helicopter and I had a dread in my entire body. I did not know what to expect and what lay waiting for us on our onward journey, but I knew it was something designed to discourage my attendance at court. There was no way I would give up on my child, regardless of what happened!

***

Twenty minutes later we approached the border of South Yorkshire and Derbyshire. The helicopter was still hovering and circling above us.

"What the hell?" I saw ahead of us blue flashing lights, then a wall of police cars; armed police officers stood in the road, forming a line across it.

"You're right—he's done something because that wall of blue lights and armed police officers are waiting for us," Spring Heeled Jack said.

"Not again! One day these idiots will realise what game he's playing.

They have too, surely. Get ready because we are obviously going to receive some sort of treatment and allegations," I replied.

The police waved down our car. An officer started toward the car, gun in full view, followed by his colleagues.

"Follow us and don't deter from where we will lead you," he growled through the window at me.

"No, I won't. What is all this about? Why should I? You have no right to treat us like this," I growled back at the officer.

The officer stared intensely at me. I could see he was annoyed, but so was I.

"I said follow us or we will arrest you," said the officer.

I took that as a threat.

"No, you won't because we have done nothing. We can go where we want. You can't stop us because we have done nothing wrong."

"That's what you say, but we are taking no risks," the officer said staring, straight at Spring Heeled Jack.

"Fuck you. I won't follow you," I hissed again.

"You either follow us to the court hearing, or you don't go at all." The officer was getting pissed at me, I could tell. I wound the window up.

"Bastards," I said out loud.

I knew that no matter how I protested this treatment the police or anyone in authority wouldn't listen to anything either my brother or I had to say. I had many times over the years heard how people described the treatment they had received at the hands of the police. I just couldn't believe this was happening to me and, worst of all, my brother. He certainly didn't need this trouble with the police, but there was nothing either of us could do about the situation.

So the convoy started from the border of South Yorkshire and Derbyshire to Chesterfield, right up to the doors at the County Court. We were waved to park the car bang outside the doors of the courthouse.

We were escorted by armed officers in a convoy of police cars; everyone stared at our vehicle.

"I hate these people. Who do they think they are? Stopping all the traffic in and around the town centre while we passed through and making an example of us! How dare they treat us this way? They have treated us and paraded us around this town as though we are some sort of dangerous criminals. Bastards!" I was furious. Spring Heeled Jack agreed and assured me it was so the police and courts couldn't be accused of not taking seriously whatever allegation Fred had made up. I instantly thought, *If they only knew what sort of man they were dealing with!*

I had learned from the previous week's experience that it was no good saying a word. I couldn't tell my family what had happened, even before all this at court started, because I suspected that some of them were unstable and capable of committing a serious crime against Fred just as Fred had committed against my mother. I previously had tried to report some of the serious crimes it was alleged Fred had committed to the police, but they just told me to do one. I felt trapped and couldn't speak to anyone. I had learned by this stage that a member of my family had attended the Chesterfield address on the morning of the first court appearance in relation to custody of my children and had indeed attacked Fred. Once I found out after I had been released from police custody, I had been furious that members of my family had taken such action against Fred. (That action itself was in dispute.) According to the police Fred had said a shot gun had been put down his throat. Family members said it was a knife, but either way it should never have happened and no one ever asked me if that's what I wanted to happen. If they had I would have told them "No" because I knew that Fred was playing me after I had attended at the Chesterfield address on the day I left, and I knew what he and Roy had done to my mother. I knew that Fred was using Roy as a human shield and I could not tell anyone.

***

The car was parked outside the courthouse and officers with guns approached the car.

"Get out and follow us. Do not stop unless we tell you to do so. Have you got that?" an officer asked.

Once outside, the car it was parked astride from the main entrance to the courthouse. In front of us were more armed police officers, staring at us as though waiting to pounce at any minute. The feeling welling up inside me was indescribable; my hatred toward the police was immense.

"Stand there!" A voice came from the back.

In front of us was a metal detector we were ordered to walk through one at a time. Spring Heeled Jack was first, and all eyes were on him from the police in attendance. Then it was my turn. As I was passing through the scanner, there to the right was Fred and one of his criminal associates known in the Chesterfield area for his skill of fighting and such.

"You bastard," I shouted toward Fred.

I was pushed in the back by an officer, "Keep moving."

I stood still on purpose. I was not going to move no matter what until I had said what I wanted to say.

"What you done now, you Grass? What lying scheming trick have you made up?"

Again I was pushed in the back .I didn't move forward; then I was pushed harder and told, "Move or get arrested. You do as we say—not as you want. Now move."

I walked as slowly as I could, still being pushed on by the police toward the courtroom where the hearing was going to be held.

I was still shouting abuse at Fred and his associate and I wasn't going to stop.

We spotted more armed police officers as we entered the courtroom. Already sat in his chair was the judge; he'd been waiting for our arrival and looking rather pissed off by it all. As I reached the front of the courtroom still surrounded by the armed officers, my solicitor rose to her feet to speak.

"You're ho..." She went to say and was immediately cut down by the judge.

"Don't bother! The mother of the child has been brought here today under armed police escort. Never in my time of being a judge have I seen such a performance. I have read the application you have submitted to this court. This application is denied and will be adjourned until another date. This mother is a very dangerous person and my view is that this is all a wasted exercise. Her sort of behaviour will not be tolerated. Case adjourned."

"What? What? What do you mean?" I shouted.

My solicitor was trying to advise me to shut up. The police stood right in front of me, looking straight at me to intimidate me.

"Are you for real?" I shouted toward the judge.

"You haven't got a clue! How dare you make such allegations about me? I've done nothing wrong and the child is mine! He should be with his mother! Whatever happened to innocent till found guilty?" I was still shouting toward the judge when two officers produced their guns for me to see.

"Bollocks, that's not going to shut me up!" I growled and turned toward Fred.

"You dirty rotten bastard! You and your friends are having a field day today, aren't you?" I spat my words with pure hatred toward Fred. I hated him and the way he was fooling everyone, and Fred and I both knew it. Fred knew that I couldn't speak to anyone or I would have done so by now. I felt so helpless and Fred loved every second.

I turned toward the officers. "You should be ashamed of yourselves." I spat my words at them.

"Take her out of this courtroom," ordered the judge, "before I detain her for contempt of court."

"Nonce," I said. I was astounded at what had just happened. We had done nothing wrong. Again we were being treated like hardened criminals. *Where was my brother?*

As I was being escorted out of the courtroom and toward the exit door I saw my brother. He hadn't been allowed into the family courtroom and he was surrounded by armed police officers. They obviously were waiting for me to come out of the courtroom. When they saw me and the armed officers coming from the courtroom the armed police started to move my brother toward the exit door so he could also be put in the car. We would be escorted out of the Derbyshire area the same way we had been brought in. Just like when we had arrived, crowds of people were looking on to see what was happening. All of it was designed to make my brother and I feel shameful. It wasn't going to work. I knew neither of us had done ought wrong. They could stare as long as they wanted; I could stare back. My brother and I were still on bail, and we had not been charged with anything, but from the treatment received from the police, we just as well had been. As I drove past all the staring people I gave them a wave, one like the queen does. That made my brother laugh.

"I don't give a fuck! They think we are important so why not act that way?" I said.

Chapter Twenty-Three
The Twisted Aggravated Burglary

The court hearings were set at different venues around the country, and when I asked why I should have to travel all over the country for my court cases I was told because the judge had ordered that all hearings to do with this case had to be listed before him. So wherever he sat on the day of any hearing I had listed, I had to go where this judge was residing. Everywhere I went I had the same reception—armed police officers, the humiliation of people standing and staring—and every time Fred attended he would give his sly grin in my direction, and I couldn't help myself but verbally have a go at him. I knew it was making things worse in the eyes of the judge, but what had I to lose? These idiots had taken my eldest son Roy and placed him with the man that had tried to murder my mother, and Roy himself had been present when this took place. The courts had been asked time and again to put my eldest son in local care. I would have asked anything to ensure Roy did not remain in Fred's care. But every time I said this to the judge he more or less told me I was "daft and over-reacting." I would sit there and think, "No, love, it's all of you that are daft!"

Having set the scene, Fred went to work in other ways during the waiting for a final custody decision. He set his sights high and caused as much damage as possible in a bid to win custody of Roy, but he hadn't applied for custody of Reggie, I wonder why? Reggie was his own son.

***

One Sunday afternoon I went to Fred's address in the Nottinghamshire area to collect my youngest son. I rounded the corner of a small road into a set of garages that sat at the back of the house Fred was renting. A friend was with me. We had just been out for the day and we were both relaxed; Fred's house was just a twenty-minute detour from the venue we had attended and now it was time for me to pick up my youngest son. As the car turned into the garages, we were met with a wall of armed police officers, guns drawn.

"For fuck's sake! What has he done now?" I said in a pissed-of sort of a way.

"Don't know, but it looks serious with this reception," answered the friend.

In a flash the police had the doors open and the occupants out. They set about searching the car and refused to answer my questions.

"What was going off?"

Then a more senior officer appeared, coming down some steps from the rear of Fred's property.

"You are under arrest for aggravated burglary," he stated.

"What? I've done nothing! I'm here to collect my son and I want him now!" I hissed.

I was really pissed off at the reception I always got from the police.

"Yes, and that's something else we need to speak to you about. But we will talk about that at the station," the officer stated.

Before I knew it I was being handcuffed and transported to the police station for questioning.

I was furious. How dare the police treat me this way? *Where was my youngest son? Why did they want to speak to me about him?* My temper was getting the better of me and I had no control over it.

"You bastards, where is my son? Is it stitch up time again? Haven't you got anything better to do, you bastards?" I was furious.

The police never said anything, never explained anything to me; they sat quiet on the onward journey to the police station.

Once inside the police station I was placed in a locked room and told someone would be in to see me shortly. The door shut with a bang.

Instantly I was transported back to all the evil crimes I was aware that Fred and accomplices had committed. I was back to the humiliation of crowds staring and the police treatment of me over the past year or so. Every time I received maximum impact from the police force and the way I was arrested, it was always like something out of the movies. I hated everyone in authority; they could do with me as they wanted and I had no control.

Somewhere within the building I kept hearing a child sobbing, like a deep groaning cry. I sat listening as the sound waxed and waned amid the noise inside the police station. I sat thinking, "Poor child, whatever is the matter? Why doesn't someone help this child?" I could tell something was seriously wrong and the sound of the crying was very disturbing.

The door to the room opened and in walked the senior officer with a man dressed in civilian clothes; I had never seen him before, but immediately I hated him. The civilian-clothed man stared at me, piercing my soul.

"What you staring at, twat?" I growled at him.

The senior officer interjected immediately, "Krisha, calm down. We are only doing our job. There is no need for that attitude."

Immediately I jumped down his throat.

"No need for attitude? I beg to differ! You and your merry men accost me and no doubt my friend. You point guns at us, and then arrest me and bring me to your fucking den. How dare you say I should not have attitude?" I could have punched him, then shook him, and shouted, "Fucking wake up," but I had no idea what was ahead for me. I just knew that whatever it was it was fabricated and maximum humility had been Fred's plan. I knew I had done nothing but felt from previous experiences that whatever the police were going to say, Fred had got the desired impact from them and it would somehow harm me in the eyes of the law.

***

I listened to what the senior officer had to say. He explained that they had received a call from Fred and he had complained to them that I had arrived at his house, produced a shot gun, robbed him of his rent and other monies, and then left the property.

The civilian-clothed man explained that he was from the NSPCC and they had also received the same call from Fred and that he was worried for the welfare of my youngest son. It was alleged that my youngest son had been in the house at the time of the alleged offence. They both went onto say that as a result of that call my youngest son had been taken into police protective custody and would remain there until this matter was resolved.

"Bollocks! What a load of bollocks! Are you people for real? Where's my son? I demand to see him now! You have no right to keep arresting me! I've done nothing wrong! Ask what you want. I've told you I have done nothing wrong and, no, I don't want a solicitor. I want to see my son!" I couldn't believe how this kept happening to me, but now it had moved another step up and my son was somewhere unknown, probably frightened to death, and both he and I were in police custody.

The questioning continued and still I insisted my innocence until finally the senior officer and the representative from the NSPPC said they would take no action this time and would take me to my son. I responded immediately, "Bollocks, this time! I've never done anything wrong! You're always harassing me. Fucking do one."

***

I walked the corridors of the police station; I could hear this groaning cry. The sound was disturbing and as I approached a door I realised it was coming from my son; I just had a gut instinct. I opened the door without being told and went inside, and there in the arms of a male police officer was my youngest son. He looked exhausted, his face hardly recognisable from all the crying he must have done. In all the years of being his mum I had never seen him like this or ever expected to either. My son turned toward the door as it opened and screamed "Mummy!" He almost collapsed but the male office caught him. I immediately went to him and we sobbed together.

"I'm sorry, Mummy. Daddy made me do it. He said he wanted me to stay with him so I told lies."

My main concern was my son. I assured him everything was going to be all right. Both he and I were allowed to go home. As I was leaving the room I spat my words at the police and the official from the NSPPC. "You bastards, look at him. Go on, look! He is only a child and you have no right to treat a boy of four like this! You should be fucking shot."

Chapter Twenty-Four
Betrayal of a Friend

I had a routine during the day while my youngest son was at school, and every day I was at the gates to meet my son from school. One day I was picking up my son and another child from school in my car with a friend. As I returned home I parked the car, when my door suddenly opened on the car and there stood a man dressed in a suit. By the time I had acknowledged the fact that the man had opened the door, he stood and read me my rights.

I was being taken to the police station for questioning. I immediately started shouting and refusing to go anywhere, but before I knew it I was outside the car and placed in handcuffs. My youngest son was looking on and crying. I couldn't get to him and I was placed in a car and whisked off to the police station.

***

Once there and after a verbal battle with the police I was finally interviewed. During the interview I was informed that Fred again had made an allegation that I had turned up at his house, threatened him with a gun, and robbed him of his money and valuables. I answered to my whereabouts and complained, as usual, that I was fed up with the false allegations and being arrested. The police didn't charge me or place me on bail but told me once they had investigated what I had said they would be back in touch. A few days later they called on the phone to say that I had nothing to answer to.

My youngest son and I were at the time residing with an old school friend of mine. We had met by chance and the friend had offered me a room. I paid our way while we were there and I contributed to the food; everything was split straight down the middle with the bills.

***

One day after taking my son to school I called back to the house to collect my training gear and swimsuit. It was the day of the week that I attended at a local sports centre with other mothers. I left for the morning training sessions and then returned back to the friend's home. I entered the bedroom I shared with my son. I noticed that something had been moved on a table in the bedroom. I knew it had been moved because before I had left that morning I had purposely put something on the table that had fallen off a bedside cabinet. I went downstairs and questioned my friend to see who had been in the bedroom. The friend said, "No one." I felt uneasy at the answer so I went back upstairs to have a look around my bedroom. I noticed that a book I had been reading had been moved and the bookmark had been put in the wrong page. I knew someone had been in the bedroom. Again I confronted my friend and again my friend denied any knowledge.

***

A month rolled on and another court hearing was coming up. The courts wanted a report on how things had been developing. My youngest son and I had just been given a local council flat. It was situated in a block across the road from the friend I had been sharing with. I had notified everyone that my son and I had moved into the flat.

One day the post arrived containing a letter sent by the solicitors who were representing me at the time. It enclosed a copy of a report that had been prepared for the courts. Contained in that report was a paragraph that stated that the police and Social Services had searched the bedroom of the house I had shared with my friend. The report continued and stated that nothing had been found when the search had been carried out, or on any of the several visits to the property. The visits had taken place so they could collate information as to my state of mind and the people I was associating with and to confirm whether I was using drugs. I was furious. How dare these people do this to me? Worst of all, my friend who I had known for years had betrayed me and I couldn't understand why. As far as I was concerned there was no problem between us and I felt betrayed. My instinct kicked in and I set out the door to confront my friend. I wanted an explanation. I found the friend at a neighbour's house and entry was refused to me. My friend wouldn't come out to speak to me.

"We will meet one day, bastard. You dirty cheating rat! Why? What have I ever done to you?" I was shouting. Everyone in the street had stopped and was staring.

"What the fuck you looking at?" I went on. "There is a dirty cheating bastard in that house and she daren't come out and explain to me why she has been doing things behind my back!" I shouted, pointing toward the house.

I headed off back toward my flat. If I had been face to face with my friend I would more than likely have hit her.

***

108

Later that morning there was a knock at the flat door. I went to answer and stood there were the Social Services. I kept them stood at the door. They informed me that they had received a telephone call from my friend, informing them of my earlier actions.

"Do one!" I told them. "You had no right to investigate me the way you have, you slimy bastards! Go fucking do your work with another that you want to stitch up. Fuck you." I slammed the door. I felt really uneasy as to why the Social Services had come. Try as I might I couldn't understand it.

***

That night the friend's estranged husband turned up at my door. I let him in saying, "It had better be good!" He had better have got a good explanation for his wife's actions. The husband went on to say that he had been contacted earlier in the afternoon by his wife. She had told him everything that had been happening and he wanted to put her side across. I sat and listened.

My friend had been approached by the police and Social Services, and they told her that I was under investigation for drugs and I was a dangerous person who they believed had possession of a gun. They had asked if they could search my room to settle the matters. She had agreed. After the search they asked if at their request could they come back and search my bedroom to rule out allegations that were being made about me. The friend knew that I was not what they were saying and that's why she had allowed it.

"Then why didn't she tell me when it had happened?" I spat.

"I don't know," he replied.

"I will tell you why. There is more to this than either of us know. One day it will come out. Things like this always have a way of rearing up at a later date," I commented.

We stood staring at each other for a few moments, and we seemed to agree telepathically on that subject.

Chapter Twenty-Five
Goodbye Was Never Said

It was a Thursday and like every day I went to pick up my youngest son from school. He had complained that a boy at school had kicked him. I was aware that there was a problem between my son and a boy in his class, and I had spoken with the school once before about it. Once we arrived home I examined my son to see if there was any bruising. I found none, and he never complained that he was in physical pain, so the night went without incident. I took my son to school the following morning. It was a Friday, and on the last school day of the week I delivered my son to school so Fred could be pick him up at the end of the day. Fred would deliver him back on a Monday morning to school for me to collect later in the afternoon. That was by order of the court. I kissed him goodbye and told him I would see him on Monday. I hated those days, but at least now I would not need to see my ex-partner any time other than at court. I always had a fear in my heart and had expressed my concerns that I felt my ex-partner would not return my son to me. I had been told over and over from the courts that this would not happen, and if I refused to obey the court orders for contact between son and father, then I would go to prison. The weekend passed without event and Monday came around. During the course of the day a friend who was going through something similar had asked for my help, but if I offered it would mean that I would not be available to collect my son from school on time. Before making a decision I contacted an old friend and asked if she could pick up my son from school. The friend said she would, so I phoned the school to notify them of the planned pick up. The headmaster answered.

"What do you mean your friend is coming to pick your son up? Haven't you heard?" said the headmaster.

"Heard? Heard what? What are you talking about?" I asked hurriedly.

"I think you need to speak to your solicitor," replied the headmaster.

"Why? Tell me what's wrong! Where is my son? There is obviously something wrong, now tell me!"

There was silence on the phone for a second or so.

"Where's my son? Tell me!" I ordered.

"I'm sorry, but it's not for me to say. You need to phone your solicitor," he replied.

"I've been in all day and I've heard nothing from my solicitor and if they needed me for something they would have contacted me. Now where's my son?"

The headmaster refused to answer my questions and kept repeating himself. I banged the phone down in temper. I had the most awful feeling in my entire body. I picked up the receiver and called to the firm of solicitors representing me at the time. I explained what had just happened on the phone with the school and demanded to know what was wrong. The solicitors had no idea and promised they would call the school and get some information then contact me back.

***

Two hours passed before I heard from the solicitor; the news was grim. The solicitor reported that Fred had obtained an emergency Residency Order over the weekend and he had secured a court order stating that my youngest son would reside with him. The solicitor had been told that my son had received an injury that had required hospital attention and that I had been given no details to the injury or which hospital my son was in because the authorities thought I had no right to know. The solicitor then went onto say that they had made an emergency application to the courts for a hearing as soon as possible so the child could be returned to me and that they were waiting as we spoke for a date and time.

"Injury? What hospital? What has happened to my son? Why haven't you got those answers? He is my son and I am his mother. I have a right to know? Court order? How's he got a court order? What has he now done?" The solicitor could not answer any of my questions. The solicitor had been prevented by the Child Protection Unit to obtain such information and would need a court order to be able to get it. The solicitor had been advised to get a court order application in with the court that day by the Child Protection Unit.

***

The court hearing came around, and I attended. An application was put to the court but before the application had been read the judge interjected the solicitor.

"Stop right there! This application has been considered and a decision as to the residency of this child has been made, and until there are some mitigating circumstances that would allow the court to consider such an application the child will stay where he is. If that's all?" the judge said.

I shot straight to my feet, my solicitor insisting that I remain mute and sit down.

"Bollocks. I'm not sitting down. That's my son and I want to know what's happened to him. Where is he? Why don't you fucking listen? You bastard, how dare you speak to my solicitor like that? I'm that child's mother and he should be with me!" I shouted.

"I advise that you listen to your counsel and sit down and stop the use of such language!" The judge stated as he was rising from his seat looking directly at me.

"You fucking nonce! Do you realise what you have done? My children are in danger and none of you can see it! Place my children in care, I beg you! Please!" I yelled at the judge. The court usher and solicitor were doing what they could to quieten me, but I was having none of it.

"You fucking nonce, do you like hurting children? You bastard!" I shouted.

The judge disappeared behind the door that he slammed when he left the courtroom. I was shouting at the top of my voice for my solicitor to do something. The solicitor just stood there silent.

"Do something—my children are in danger!" I shouted.

The solicitor stood mute.

"You're fucking sacked! Hear me? Sacked! Get out of my sight! You're all fucking daft! My children are in danger and you have let this happen. How could you?" I shouted, demanding an answer. Security was in the courtroom by this stage. They were approaching me and asking that I leave the building.

"Go fuck yourself, bastards! They have placed my children in danger. They are all fucking paedophiles! Come one step nearer and I will smash your fucking faces right in!" I was going mental but meant every word.

Eventually I left the courtroom, and till I left the building I was shouting at the top of my voice that all judges were nonces and that my children had been kidnapped. I never let up and everyone just stood silent looking at me. For the first time in all the months I had been treated like a villain I was now acting like one and I didn't give a fuck.

***

Once outside I collapsed in a heap in the car park and broke down and sobbed uncontrollably. No one came to my aid. I don't know if anyone even noticed. My world had been shattered into so many pieces; how my life would continue I had no idea. The legal system had taken my life and, worse, my children's life. I had never been questioned about any allegations from the police. The system had decided that whatever the crime had been reported I was guilty and it deserved my children being removed from my care.

I just kept assuring myself that one day someone would open their eyes and my children would be returned to me. They must do!

***

At a later date I was interviewed by the police at my insistence in relation to an assault on my youngest son. During the interview I was questioned as to whether I owned certain items of footwear.

When I said "No" the police confirmed to me that they had without my consent or knowledge searched my home and spoke to several people I knew. They admitted they knew I had not committed any crime, but they stated that they were acting under different sets of laws and the law that allowed interviewing me at that time could not be given in evidence in the family courtroom unless they were ordered to do so by a judge.

***

The months rolled on and no matter where I went for legal advice I was told the same thing: unless there was something for the courts to consider in relation to my children's residence, then there was no way I could approach the courts. My legal representatives told me that it didn't matter that I had been interviewed about an assault on my youngest son and then been released without charge. The courts would have taken into account that I had not been interviewed or charged with an offence when the courts had come to a decision that one of my children had received an injury that warranted hospitalisation while under my care. I was so frustrated. I couldn't understand no matter how much I questioned everything how the courts could justify removing my youngest son when I had done nothing wrong. I heard what legal advice I had been given, but I knew it was all wrong! Did this happen to other people? Were they as frustrated as I was? Was this how our great British legal system treats its subjects? There was definitely something wrong. I had no contact at all with my children, even though a court order was made saying I could have unlimited contact. No one would listen or act when I contacted official agencies. They didn't want to know how unfairly I was being treated. I received the same reply every-where I went, "Go back to court! We cannot make the children see you or make your ex-partner allow you to see your children! He has a court order and he is not bound by any rules!"

Could you believe it? He was bound by no court order but I had been threatened with prison if I stopped contact between father and son! Never once throughout all this time had I seen Roy by way of contact. I had only ever seen him when he had attended court with my ex-partner. He never acknowledged me in anyway, only when he made false allegations of my treatment toward him whenever we may have passed by one another or I found myself in the same part of a court building that he was in.

No one ever made sure that court orders in relation to him were carried through. When I complained of my treatment from Roy to official people they never said or did anything. He had free run of destroying my life and adding to the unwarranted pressure that was being placed upon me. He was helping to secure the removal of my youngest son by way of remaining with Fred and contributing to false allegations made about me.

I was being backed more and more into a corner. Everyone's actions, decisions, recommendations, and even court orders where aimed against me all the time. It didn't matter what I said or did—everything was a waste of time. But there was no way I was going to stop fighting for my children, regardless of how my children's minds had been corrupted. I was innocent of everything.

Chapter Twenty-Six
The Telephone Account

I received a phone call from a Nottinghamshire police force asking if they could come and see me, and if I didn't agree then they would come and arrest me to question me. The police explained they didn't want to take that course of action against me.

The police attended at my home address. The officer introduced himself and got straight down to business.

"Do you have a telephone account?"

"Yes you know I have—you contacted me on my telephone number. Why?" I asked.

"Do you have more than one telephone contract with your service provider or any other provider?" the officer asked.

"No. Why?" I replied, getting annoyed.

"I would like to show you a document for a contract held with BT. You will see that the account is held in your name. Is that your signature?" asked the officer.

I looked at the document. The information contained on the paper was an account held in my name. The telephone number was for the area of Nottinghamshire.

"That is not my signature! However, it looks like it and the information on the contract that is attached to this document holds all my personal information. I can assure you I have no phone contract apart from the one I have at my home address where we are now." I looked at the officer.

"Is this where my children live? "I asked.

I held my stare on the officer. The officer did not answer my question, so I tried questioning him again, but still he refused to answer. But the officer continued to question me.

"Have you had or do you have any dealings with a firm of solicitors in the Nottingham area?"

"Yes, I have previously. Why?" I asked.

"Please. Just answer the questions, and once we are done I will try to answer whatever I can. OK?" the officer said to me.

The questioning continued and I was asked if I knew a certain female employee at the firm of the solicitors I had used in the past. I told the officer I did not.

The crime the office was investigating started to unfold. An account in my name had been opened at a house in the Nottinghamshire area at the address stated on the agreement. The phone number had been traced after an employee at the firm of solicitors I had previously used in the Nottingham area had made a complaint to the police that she was receiving nuisance calls with a sexual nature. The calls at times had become very stressful and the police agreed that a criminal act had taken place and someone should be held responsible for their actions.

"So what do you want me to do? I don't know anything about any of this! What can I do?" I asked the officer.

The officer asked me if I would make a statement to that effect. I agreed.

Once the statement had been completed the officer told me that they knew that Fred was responsible for the calls and they intended to charge him with the offence. I never heard any more from the police in relation to this matter. But from my experience of living with Fred and all the allegations from known associates of Fred's crimes and partners in the past, I knew that Fred would have committed the said crime.

Around the same time my youngest son's behaviour had started to worsen in relation to doing as he was told. I had spoken to my solicitor about his behaviour he had become almost impossible at times to cope with. He wanted more and more to spend time at the friend's house. I was uneasy with this, but my son had bonded with the friend's daughter and they played together all the time. This really made conversation hard for me with my old school friend, but my son still needed his social life, limited as it was.

One day I saw the friend's daughter out playing.

"Hello, will you be going to the police station this weekend? I know that Fred is going to make a lie up about you, saying that you have frightened him so much they are having to live and sleep in a friend's cellar!" the little girl said.

I had no intention of answering the question and just changed the subject. Then I made my way to my ex-friend's house to enquire over the comment passed by her daughter.

"Why has your daughter just asked me if I'm going to the police station this weekend? She tells me that Fred and my kids are living in a cellar! So if your daughter's heard something then you will have! So what's this all about?" I asked the friend.

"I haven't a clue! Wha...."The friend was cut off by her daughter.

"Yes Mummy! You know when Fred phoned and told you! We were all sat down watching T.V. in the room and when he phoned you put her son on the phone to talk to his dad. Then you spoke to him and after we all sat talking about what lies he was going to tell!" the little girl insisted.

"No! I don't know what you're talking about," the friend said to her daughter.

The little girl went to speak again, but I had heard enough.

"It doesn't matter! I now know where my true friends lie and it is not at this door," I said, glaring at the friend.

I was so angry. *Why? Why was my friend lying to me?* I knew the little girl knew what she was talking about, but there was no way I could act on the information I had just received. It was a weekend and I had no way of contacting the solicitor. I would have to sit and wait till Monday to contact the solicitor and explain what I had found out. The weekend passed without incident but I was as jumpy at any noise. I was expecting something to happen, but I didn't know what. The feeling was really getting to me and I could barely eat. Every time I did I felt sick. If I drank tea or coffee I felt the same. The weekend dragged on. On Monday I contacted the solicitor and everything that I had learned from the little girl I told my solicitor. The only thing that I was advised to do was just sit back and wait for whatever to happen. That was not what I had expected and I started shouting, saying the solicitor needed to do something. I didn't know what he could do, but it couldn't go on like this. The solicitor said they were helpless and until something happened they too would have to sit and wait.

***

I didn't have to wait too long. Monday afternoon about mid-day someone knocked on the door. Social Services! Just as I had been informed by the little girl days earlier, they had come to see me with view to a complaint they had received from Fred. He was alleging that he couldn't remain in the house he occupied because I was terrorising him and he had to take to living in a friend's cellar to ensure his own safety and that of the children. I told them none of the allegations were true and asked why was it every time Fred made an allegation I was always threatened or investigated?

I went on to say that nothing that I had ever been accused of was true and that they should open their eyes! I had said this many times before and, like always, it fell on death ears. By the look on their faces, I knew they didn't believe a word I was saying. It was explained that my solicitor had been contacted only that day and given the details of the little girl's statement to me. I stated that now it appears everything the little girl had said was apparently true! The Social Services didn't answer but then made quickly their excuses and left. I knew there was no point in arguing with them. They were out to believe everything Fred said. I would never be believed.

Chapter Twenty-Seven
The Children Are Ill

A year or so had passed since I had last seen my youngest son. I had given up hope that I would ever see Roy again. After more court reports it was clear my eldest had completely lost his respect and love for me. And from what I had been reading in the reports, my youngest son appeared to be heading in the same direction, but there was no way I would stop fighting for my children. I had done nothing wrong and to stop fighting in my eyes was like an admission of guilt—and that was never going to happen.

I was still engaged in battles between the Social Services and CasCas. Their reports spoke of what other people's opinions were in relation to the case at hand. They contained recommendations of what they thought should take place and never once did those recommendations have me and the care I could give to my children in them. They did include my adamant protests of my children being kidnapped and denial of any wrongdoing to my children on my behalf. The reports made it perfectly clear that the recommendations were to leave the children with Fred.

***

It was my birthday and I had gone out for a meal in the early evening with a friend, returning home about 8 o'clock. As I pulled up in my car outside my home, I could hear the phone ringing indoors. There was no point rushing because I wouldn't get to it in time, and there was an answer-phone on the machine. Once I was settled inside I would listen to see if there was a message and contact the person back if necessary. As I was walking up the drive I heard the phone go again. I turned to my friend and said, "Well someone wants me!" We laughed. By the time we had reached the door the phone had stopped. We got inside and took off our coats and the phone rang again.

"Someone definitely wants me. Sorry, just let me get it," I said to my friend.

I answered the call. It was one of my sisters, Ellen, and what she had to say really upset me. As the conversation unfolded my sister explained that she had received a call from Fred. He had told her there was something wrong with my kids and he needed to see me immediately. He went onto say that he had contacted loads of my friends and had got their numbers from an address book I had left in my home that he remained in while I had lived at Chesterfield. My sister asked for a contact number, and he had left one, stating it was a matter of emergency. Since the call she had continuously been trying to contact me. I looked down at the answerphone indicator and it said I had received thirty messages. I took the number down and said once I had found out what it was about I would phone my sister back and tell her what the problem was.

I tried the number I had been given, it was a mobile number, but the network stated there was no such number. Obviously some number had been placed in the wrong place or one was missed out. I called back and explained to my sister and stated that first thing in the morning I would contact my solicitor and get them to find out what the problem was. I still had not had contact with my children in any form.

The following morning I contacted my solicitor and explained the previous night's message, stating that several people over the course of the night had contacted me with the same message. When others had asked for a contact number, Fred had said he had left his number with my sister.

A few hours passed and the solicitor called me back. She had spoken with Fred's solicitor and they had said they would contact their client and get back in touch. They had, and now the solicitor was passing the contact number to me. The solicitors had no idea what had happened or what concerns there were with the children, and Fred had refused any details to his solicitor. I took the number and explained that once I knew what was wrong I would get back in touch with the solicitor.

I managed to reach Fred, but we only arranged a place to meet; he promised he would explain everything to me then. I immediately contacted my solicitor and explained everything that had been said. The solicitor advised that if I was to go to the arranged meeting place then I should contact the police in that area and notify them, giving contact details if they needed to confirm anything.

Later that day I arrived at the destination, which wasn't that far away from my house. Fred was already there, sitting in a car. As I pulled up and parked Fred got out and came to my car.

"Where are my children?" I growled at him. I had a fear that something terrible had happened. Why was Fred there without the children? I thought.

"Oh, they are OK" Fred replied.

"Then why am I here? You said there was something wrong with my children, you evil bastard. You did that to make me come to meet you, didn't you?"

"No—I do need to speak to you about the children," he came to his defence. "But this is not the place to talk about it. Can we go to my house?" he asked me.

"Bollocks! Do you think I'm daft? So you can set me up for something? No! Where are my children? "I growled again.

"I promise no tricks or set ups. I just need to speak to you about them and I don't want to do it here," he said.

"No. I can't trust you," I answered.

"Then contact your solicitor or the police if you want to tell them, but here is not the place, please!" he said.

After contacting both the police and solicitor I followed Fred to a house not far from my own. This is where Fred and my children now lived. The house was empty when we arrived. Once settled with a cuppa I pushed Fred for an explanation.

"So now, tell me what's wrong with my children?" again growling at him.

He went on to say that he had been ill and couldn't cope with the care of the children on his own and asked that I take an active part seeing that I didn't live that far away from them. He went onto say that the police had kept him informed of where I was living and that's why he thought this would make sense.

"Fuck you! After everything you have done to me and mine, you think I am going to forget what you have done? You tried to kill my mother, you have stolen my children, and now you want to wave a white flag. No! No! No! If you can't cope with my children, then I suggest you contact your solicitor so that it can go to court and be dealt with the proper way," I spat at him.

A noise came from the kitchen; we both looked toward the door in the living room. I was sitting on a sofa straight across from the door opening. Roy had just walked past the door opening and had not looked in the room at all. There was Reggie following closely behind. In those split seconds I could tell how much my children had changed. A second later Reggie had backed up and was looking at me sat on the sofa.

"Mummy, Mummy it's you! Oh mummy, I miss you," shouted Reggie.

In a split second Roy was in the doorway.

"Mum, I didn't recognise you. I miss you, Mum." He was on the sofa arms, around my neck, and he was crying.

With both children in tears and obviously heartbroken I turned to look at Fred. He showed no emotion. It was like the whole thing wasn't happening.

"Happy now?" I spat at Fred.

He never flinched. The children clung to me so tightly that I could hardly breathe. While I was at the house they followed me around like my shadow. Fred broached the question again about me helping with the care of the children. Over the next few weeks I attended at Fred's house to take my children to school and pick them back up.

Fred offered me a newer car, one that he was driving. The only way I would accept would be if Fred wrote and signed a piece of paper stating he had given me the car. I had experienced everything of the worst sort with Fred and there was no way I would trust him with his offer and I told him so. Fred didn't hesitate; he wrote the letter saying he would do whatever he had to put right the wrong he had done. In my mind he could never do that. He had attempted to murder my mother and I felt he was the cause of her death—that could never be changed. He had turned my own children against me. They had told lies and had reported they didn't want anything to do with me—how could that ever be changed?

One day while I was in the kitchen preparing a meal for my children Fred approached me from behind and put his arm around my waist. I immediately pushed him away and he tried again, this time a bit more forceful. That was it. I lashed out at him with the heel of my foot. Crack! I had broken something, and I was relieved that Fred had let go of me. An argument broke out between us. I grabbed my car keys and left the property. There was no way I could stay there any longer. I could now see Fred for what he was really up to and there was no way I would ever let that happen. By the time I had left Fred's property and arrived at my own house I had received ten voicemails on my mobile phone and several text messages, all threatening that I would pay a great cost for leaving his house, the children, and him. I went to the police station and had the calls and text recorded. I knew how Fred worked after everything I had been through, and there was no way I was going to ignore the serious threats that had been contained in his messages—things like, I would go to prison for the rest of my life and I would never see my children ever again. Once I had finished at the police station I returned home and made arrangements to go stay at a friend's out of town.

When I returned to my home after staying away a couple of nights, I had no sooner got in and there was a knock on the door. It was a neighbour calling to ask where I had been and explaining that for the past few days the police had questioned almost everyone on the road to my whereabouts and recent activity. He couldn't tell me anything more. I knew Fred had done something, but it no longer came as a shock. He was playing true to his colour. But the only thing I was going to do was sit and wait for the police to come. I didn't have to wait long. After answering the door to a knock I was tackled to the floor; sniffer dogs entered the house with their handlers and a fat female PC sat on my back. A pair of shoes stopped right in front of my face.

"Are you going to behave yourself if I let you stand up?" It was a man's voice.

"Go fuck yourself, twat! Do what you want—you usually do! Anything that Grass says you over-react, so just get on with it, twat!" I spat my words.

"Now listen here, I have not come here for a war with you. I'm just doing my job! Promise to behave and I will have the handcuffs removed and you stood on your feet," the voice came back.

"How about do one?" I snapped back.

In an instant and without warning I was hauled to my feet and was stood facing a man in a suit.

"Now listen to me! I'm not here to start a war with you. A crime has been reported to us and it's my job to investigate that crime. Now I'm not going to fall out with you. I just want to speak to you about the alleged crime and your whereabouts, OK?" he said.

"Bollocks and do one, twat!" I hissed.

The officer continued. He ordered that the handcuffs be removed and asked if he could sit down while we spoke. I stared at him. I could see through the window to the back garden, and there were police officers with dogs all over the garden.

"Why are their police dogs and officers all over my house and back garden?" I asked the officer.

"If you're now prepared to listen, I will explain," the officer said.

It unfolded that an allegation of attempted murder had been made by Fred and that there was a witness to the event —Roy —who had identified me as the person responsible. There was also a complaint that I had stolen Fred's car.

I knew that whatever it was that Fred had over my son was by far more evil an experience than attempting to kill his grandmother and now stitching up his mother for attempted murder.

I was transported to the police station. Once I arrived I was placed in a room and told that I would be interviewed as quickly as they could get to me. When I asked why I was told that Fred and Roy were also at the police station and they were making statements. Once these statements had been obtained the questioning would then take place.

"What a load of bollocks!" I sighed.

It was nine o'clock at night before the police were in position to interview me. I was taken from a detention room to a Porta Kabin where I was interviewed. The office told me of the allegation.

Apparently Fred had been in his living room when Fred and I started to argue. Fred alleged that I had run at him with a syringe in my hand and stabbed him in the leg. He alleged that shortly after he couldn't remember anything. Roy alleged he was sitting on the stairs and he could see us both clearly. He confirmed what Fred was saying, adding that I had taken Fred's car. At some time after the alleged offence the police were called and a complaint was made. This complaint had led to the arrest of myself and that's why the police were searching everywhere in my house—they were looking for drugs of any description. The officer explained that since the complaint had been raised they had been trying to locate me and a neighbour had called to the police station to report that I had returned home. Because of the nature of the complaint it was being treated as "serious."

I asked the officer if he believed the bollocks that had been reported and he replied, "It's my job to investigate the reported crime, not to have an opinion." I was asked to account for the reason I had left Fred's house and my whereabouts while the police had been trying to locate me, Fred's car, and the allegation of theft of his vehicle, and then finally make a statement to that effect. After everything had been done I was bailed and asked to attend back at the police station in a month. The reason for this the officer said was that blood samples had been taken from Fred and sent to the police forensic labs. The result of those test needed to be establish before any further action could be taken in relation to the reported crime.

Before the month was up for me to answer bail to the police station the officer in charge of the case called me to tell me not to bother surrendering for bail as the blood test results were back and they were negative for what they were looking for. The officer also said that he had shown Fred a letter that he had written in his own hand and signed, stating that he was giving ownership of the car to me. Fred had said he could not remember doing it so the officer had pointed out to Fred that Fred had made a correction on the letter and had he not been able to remember he certainly would not have made the said correction. The officer informed me that Fred had stated that he would make a complaint about the police for not acting seriously and arresting me. He advised that Fred had stated that he would get his car back and would go through the county courts.

He advised me that I should stay away from my children and accept they were a danger to me and they couldn't be rescued from Fred and the control he had over them. They were a lost cause, so to speak.

Chapter Twenty-Eight
County Court

Within a matter of weeks a summons to appear at the county court was delivered to my house. Fred had made an application to the court wanting the car back. A hearing date and time had been set. I considered taking legal action but thought against it because I had been through enough with solicitors and legal people. I just thought I could represent myself. That's exactly what I did.

On the morning of the hearing I turned up at court at the set time. While I sat in the foyer of the courthouse I could hear Fred somewhere in the building; as usual he was making some demand of some poor legal adviser, his voice echoing around the building. Then I noticed the voice was coming from the landing above and making its way to the staircase within the building. I looked up to the top of the staircase and there was Fred shouting and demanding. As the party proceeded down the staircase I looked at Fred.

"Pond life," I said out loud, making sure Fred and his party heard me.

I just couldn't help myself. This immediately got a reaction from Fred and again he was hurling abuses at me, making all sorts of allegations at the top of his voice, but I just sat there staring straight at him.

The usher came from a doorway a few minutes later and called my name. I made the usher aware of whom I was and in turn was told the hearing was due to start. I was asked to follow the usher into the room.

Sat waiting for Fred and his party to enter the room, I was surprised when Fred entered on his own. The judge residing started the case by explaining what the case was about and what the plaintiff was requiring from the defendant. The judge then informed both parties that the case was being recorded and asked Fred to start his case. It was the biggest load of rubbish I had heard, and like he complained to the police there he was stating the same thing to the judge. He was angry and it showed. He stated that I had injected him so he didn't know what he was doing. He had written and signed a letter stating he was handing ownership of the said vehicle to me while drugged. He stated that if he had been *cosmos mentis*, then that would never have happened. He also said that Roy had witnessed it all and together they had approached the police to make a complaint about the whole incident. The judge interjected at that point saying, "for the purpose of the tape the police have investigated your allegation and no charges have been brought." Immediately Fred came to his own defence, stating he had made a complaint to the police complaints department and it was still being looked at. Fred called his first and only witness—Roy. The same story unfolded; Roy was very convincing, I must say. Being so young is what Fred had banked on, hoping that the court would take the view that no child in his right mind would make a statement to the police about their mother attempting to murder someone and then come to court under oath. Fred finished presenting his case. The judge then ordered that I give my version of accounts. I rose to my feet.

"I have a question for this witness."

"You state that you witnessed the whole incident and that you had a perfect view of the whole incident?" I asked Roy.

"Yes! Yes I did. And you attempted to murder Fred. I was there. I saw everything and I went with Fred to the police station to report the crime," Roy snapped back.

I took a moment to look at my son. I knew there was no hope; this child has been brainwashed and I now knew Fred had some sort of hold over this child because I had done nothing yet again. I would need to take another account of everything my son had said.

"Can I ask you a question and you give me an honest answer?" I asked.

"Yes, you can, but I will still tell you the same thing—you tried to murder Fred you know it and so do I," he growled back at me, his stare intense. His body language was threatening.

"OK. Well here we go then. Remember you said that you would answer honestly," I said.

"Yes, I will, and you know that I'm telling the truth anyway," he snapped again.

Good, I thought. I now have him worked up. I can see from his body language that he has been prepared for anything that might be asked of him.

"Right, let me ask you this. If you were walking in the park with your Nan-nan and someone grabbed and stole her bag, then ran off, leaving your Nan-nan shocked and shaken, what would you do?" I asked.

"Which Nan-nan?" answered Roy.

I now knew I had him. He thought that by that answer and stalling for time he would place me back at the scene of my mother's attempted murder site. *Clever.*

"Your nan-nan Martha, of course," I answered.

"What would I do? I would run after that person and if I couldn't catch them I would immediately call the police," he said in a cold voice and staring straight through me.

It's no wonder he hasn't died from pneumonia with the ice inside his soul.

"Are you sure about that?" I asked.

"Yes! Yes I'm sure that if anyone did that to my nan-nan I would do what I have just said without a shadow of a doubt." He looked cold and convincing.

"To be honest with you I don't believe you would." I led him along.

"I have told you and this court. I would do exactly what I say, and I wouldn't hesitate." He spat the answer through his teeth.

He was getting annoyed at being questioned about his loyalty to his family and I could see straight through him. I had enough experience of both my son and Fred over the years.

"Then can you tell the court why you didn't phone the police immediately when, as you allege, you saw I was trying to kill Fred?" I said this steadily and deliberately in a cold tone, ensuring he would respond in the desired manner.

"You bastard! You bastard! You have tricked me!" he shouted through the tears of his frustration.

He had realised what he had said, and he now knew their lies had been uncovered. He rose to his feet and ran from the courtroom. Arms flailing and sobbing, he disappeared out of sight. Fred immediately rose to his feet.

"You're a bastard! A bastard! Do you hear me? What mother would do such a thing to her son? Questioning him like that? You tried to murder me and you know it," Fred was shouting as he was kicking the chair away from himself. His arms were waving all over the place; he was almost spitting his words and he too ran from the courtroom. The room fell silent for a moment.

Then the judge turned to face me, saying, "I could not have executed that any better myself. Well done! We will wait a moment to see if anyone comes back and then I will make my direction in this matter."

We both sat in a nearly silent room; you could hear voices that were raised but couldn't make out what was being said. Fred returned about ten minutes later; he was shouting at the top of his voice and he thought his intimidation would have the impact he was hoping for. He wasn't prepared for the outcome that followed. The judge found that Fred had given the car as a present and when he had not gotten the desired outcome with me, he and his witness had falsified their story. The car would remain with me.

Fred went through the roof, shouting all sorts of abuse at the judge. The judge, like me, just sat there and listened to everything Fred had to say. The judge turned to me and told me I could leave the court now. I rose to my feet and walked straight past Fred and out of the door.

Chapter Twenty-Nine
The Final Court Order

After almost three years the final hearing came around in relation to the residence of my children.

The judge said that it was the only case that he had dealt with in all his career where the mother had been under investigation for almost three years and no charges had ever been brought. "The mother has had her identity turned inside out and been accused of the most heinous crimes, and she is innocent of everything. It is with regret that I have to make this order, but my job is to take into consideration everyone involved and that includes the children. The children keep stating that they want to live with their father, and taking into account their ages I have to listen to what they are saying. I make an order that both children live with the father, but the mother can have unlimited access with no supervision. She will receive regular photos and copies of all school reports. I understand that the mother did not want this outcome, but this case has to be brought to an end." Immediately I was on my feet.

"You fucking nonce! You have sentenced my children to a life of crime. They are being emotionally abused. You can see that and so can I! You just don't give a fuck about my children, but I do. I've asked repeatedly for the courts to take my children into care to protect them from that evil bastard and no one is listening." I was shouting at the top of my voice and looking around the courtroom while I was shouting. The courtroom was full: barristers, legal representatives, solicitors. When my gaze met theirs they turned their faces away.

"You bastards! You fucking bastards. Their lives are going nowhere fast. How can you do this to my children?"

Everyone's head was hung down as I looked round the room again. The only person who held their head high was the judge who had made the order. I knew from experience with the family courts over the years that my words were falling on death ears. I walked toward the front of the court, looked at the judge, and called him a nonce. Everyone just stood there.

The judge was just looking at me. I turned around and headed for the door of the courtroom, knocking paperwork from the benches that legal representative had in front of them for upcoming cases that morning. As I reached the door I kicked it open, spun around one more time and yelled, "I hope each and every one of you can live with your fucking selves. You fucking nonces." You could have heard a pin drop within the entire building. Everyone now on the outside of the courtroom was looking at me, but I carried on shouting.

"My children have been kidnapped and those nonces have allowed it."

***

I never saw or heard from my children ever again. I had verbal battles with Social Services, who were supposed to ensure I got the ordered contact. I was told that Fred had left town with no forwarding address, and therefore they were not bound to find where he had gone. He was not a criminal and could take the children wherever he wanted. I had been cheated yet again by the system. No one wanted to know. I would turn up at the Social Services at Christmas and birthdays for the first couple of years of not knowing where my children were and was turned away every time. They would not take the presents or pass anything on to my children. I had applied for legal aid in a bid to track my children's whereabouts, but the legal aid board said they would not fund any application in relation to my children and that the previous court cases had cost enough. Even though at the time I wasn't working they would not fund anything. There was no real possibility that I would ever get my children back in my life.

***

Years passed on and I saved enough to fund an application before the courts in relation to no contact. A date and time were set in a part of the country where the children were residing: Mansfield, Nottinghamshire. Fred didn't turn up to the court, and an order was made that he should be fetched before the courts to answer why he had not attended. The court official who had attended at their home address informed the court that Fred had left his known home address with no forwarding address, and at the time of the hearing they had not been able to locate him or the children. Weeks passed and finally I received notification from the court that a hearing had been set. I employed a local firm of solicitors to attend the hearing with me.

The hearing didn't go without incident, but that was no shock to me. I knew Fred and knew exactly what to expect and I wasn't let down by him or Roy.

The court witnessed Fred's behaviour. He was true to form—same old Fred, same old tricks. Nothing had changed—still the aggression and still the same old allegations and more on top. An order was made that a report would be made for the court. A further date was set.

***

The date came around again. I was aware that now everyone had been seen and a report had been prepared for the judge to consider. I was furious when I read the report; the recommendation was that Fred's wishes should be considered, and the fact that I had not seen the children for years was quiet upsetting for the family as a whole. While everyone was waiting to go into the courtroom Fred and Roy again were true to form, causing a scene outside the courtroom.

We went into court and Fred was yet again throwing the chair back and shouting his lies again. The judge asked him to be quiet, but he wouldn't listen. He stormed out of the room, leaving the judge, the legal representative, and me silent. The judge looked at me; he apologised for Fred's behaviour and asked if I still wanted to go on with the application. He reminded me of all the years that everyone had gone through during the hearings until the final order was made. He asked me to seriously consider. I quoted to the judge a sentence from the court report where my youngest son had told the court official he wanted to see his mum but his dad wouldn't let him. The judge reminded me of all the trouble that would surround my youngest son if he was allowed to see his mother. I was back in an instant to all the years and all the allegations that Fred and Roy had created. I had to make a decision on what course of action needed to be taken. Sitting silent I thought of the entire trauma that had already been in both my sons' lives.

I advised the judge to drop the application. The judge told me it would be best for my youngest son all around because he would not have the pressure placed upon him by his father. I had the sentence running around in my head that I had read in the report. It read, "I want to see my mum. I want to know her but my dad won't let me." Based on that sentence I decided instantly that one day my youngest son would come looking for me, and now I knew at last that I had gotten the message home to him that I wanted him in my life. I decided it would be a matter of years, but one day he would come and I would be waiting. The judge made the order that my application was denied.

I left the courthouse with mixed feelings. I knew from the behaviour of Fred and Roy that they believed they had been triumphant yet again. Little did they know that I had been asked by the judge as to what course of action he should take and it had been my decision.

I could leave the courthouse knowing for the first time in all the years that had passed that I had been consulted, and I knew in my heart my youngest son would come to me. I needed to keep those thoughts with me until the day came that my son and I would be reunited.

Chapter Thirty
The Years in Between
the Final Court Order
for Residency

During those years I had been under the care of two doctors, and I had repeatedly told them how ill I was feeling. I had test after test, and every time except once they all came back normal. I was told that there was something wrong with my thyroid, and it needed to be kept an eye on. The doctor wasn't alarmed, so why should I be? My symptoms were always present and I had lost loads of weight. It was quiet upsetting feeling so ill and no proper diagnosis.

***

While living in the Sheffield area I was the victim of a series of assaults from members of my own family. From what I knew at the time some of them had been incarcerated with Fred and had a disliking to him. Some of my family members were opposed to the fact I was trying to see Roy while he lived with Fred, so they took it upon themselves to attack me for daring to attempt to see him.

I will list here some of the incidents that took place. The added pressure was unbearable at times. How I coped I will never understand myself, let alone ask anyone else to try and understand the mental and physical torture I went through.

Someone attempted to set fire to my flat. Having gone out for the night, I left the light on in the property, giving the illusion that the flat was occupied. When I returned the next day I found that someone had tried to set fire to my main door.

A few days later I was awoken by a neighbour to show me that someone had put graffiti all over my car.

All these incidents were reported to South Yorkshire police, and in turn the police visited at least one member of my family because they knew for definite he was responsible for the car vandalism. A year earlier that member had assaulted me, all because I had contact with Roy who was living with Fred and the member didn't like Fred and thought I should not see my son or Fred. When I stood up to the bully, he repeatedly hit me about the head with his fists, causing an injury that needed hospital attention and a possible operation because of the extent of the injury. I refused to have the operation and signed myself out of the hospital. The member of the family had been sentenced to a term in prison. When the attack on the car took place the member had just been released from prison.

Many times when I returned home from outings my neighbours would tell me that a small group of men had visited my flat and had been banging hard and loudly on my door and shouting threatening abuse through the letterbox.

I came back to my flat after spending the night at a friend's house and found that my front door had been beaten down and that threatening graffiti was written on the inside wall of my flat.

At this point I left the Sheffield area and the police assisted me.

***

The following incidents I had no idea about at all. I had no idea why these incidents were happening, and it took a few more years before I could finally piece together why they occurred.

I was being contacted by my friends from Sheffield, explaining that they had been physically attacked and had been asked where I was. When they had refused to say because they didn't know my whereabouts, they were subjected to terrifying ordeals of physical violence and ghost rides.

Spring Heeled Jack was attacked by a local drug dealer and his associates; they were trying to find out my whereabouts. They cut his throat and repeatedly told him the vile acts they were going to perform on me once they found where I was. They told him they were going to murder me and sexually assault me because I was taking over their drug patch and that no one does that to them.

They attacked my niece. She was walking to the shop with her new baby in the pushchair when she was grabbed from the pavement, dragged into a car, and held with a knife to her throat by a brother of the drug baron. This brother had AIDS, and he held a knife to his wrist above her mouth that was being forced open by another gang member and threatened to infect her with the AIDS virus if she did not tell them where I was. The baby was left in the pushchair unattended while the mother was subjected to the physical attack.

A lifelong friend had gone to the chemist to get baby food for her young daughter and was approached and threatened by the drug gang members; they gave her a message to pass to me that once they found my whereabouts they would kill me. Information was given to the friend of my car's make and registration; they explained that my nephew had supplied them with those details and it would only be a matter of time.

A number of friends throughout the south Yorkshire region were visited by the drug baron and his associates. They were threatened with acts of violence if it was found that they knew my whereabouts and were not telling.

The drug baron and his associates attended at my great niece's funeral with a bid of finding me there. Everyone at the funeral was asked why I had not attended the funeral. Threats were again sent out to me and my life, stating that I would soon be found by them.

During this time, I was in touch with the police. The police were asking me to get people to go to them and complain. No one was willing to do that because of the threats they had received. There was only one person who spoke to the police—my brother, Spring Heeled Jack. I contacted him after hearing of the attack against him. He spoke to the police over the telephone and said he did not want to press charges against them, but he knew that whatever it was that these people thought I was guilty of, I would not be involved.

***

While all these things were happening to me I was receiving regular arrests from members of various police forces in connection to the complaints they were receiving from Fred and Roy. The pressure of all the activities was mounting up on top of me and my health was taking a serious battering. My weight plummeted. I was down to nine stone and my energy levels were virtually non-existent. I was now under the care of a new doctor, and, like the one previous, he carried out routine checks only to come back saying everything was normal. The doctor advised that I eat more. But I was eating OK, so between us we thought it must be stress related.

***

In addition to all of this, the court officials were writing in their court reports for the judge's information all activity surrounding me at that time. I complained furiously to my legal representatives, but they told me there was nothing they could do. I asked if I could oppose what was being written because some of the findings were simply not true. I was told, "No, there is no facility for you to do that." People were saying and doing things that I had no control over. During this period I sacked more legal representatives, and it all felt like a helpless cause. I wished at times that I were dead. I was the person at the centre of the legal reports, the criminal accusations, and the head hunting by the drug baron, and I was guilty of nothing. Life couldn't get much worse for me. Knowing everything I did and not being able to speak about it was the worst feeling in the world. I felt like I was going mental.

During this period I had met a new man that I had formed a relationship with. I knew little about his past other than he had five children and they didn't live in the South Yorkshire area. This didn't concern me; many people like me were parted from their children and if life had taught me one thing, shit happens beyond your control sometimes. After a few months of getting to know this man he suggested that I meet his family. I didn't want to do this. I felt uneasy introducing new people into my life—there were enough people digging into my life without more being added to the list—but I took on board Dustin's wishes and a date was set for me to go meet his family.

Disaster struck immediately I entered the mother's property and sat there in the lounge was another man, Jimmy, who I had been involved with briefly but I had ended the relationship due to the pressure I had and was still under about a year previous. Jimmy had not wanted to end the relationship and had tried really hard to convince me otherwise. As soon as our eyes met and the realisation struck home I turned around and made for a quick exit.

"What's up?" everyone in the house was asking, watching me putting my shoes on as quickly as I could.

"Hello." Jimmy entered the hallway. "How you keeping?" Jimmy was staring hard at me. I felt immediately uncomfortable with this situation.

"Do you know her?" said Jimmy's new girlfriend.

"Know her? Know her? I should. This is the woman that I love," Jimmy replied.

I just wanted to fall through a hole in the floor. Embarrassment was not the word! I was being urged to stay by everyone. I didn't really want to, but they made it really difficult for me. Everyone wanted answers and I did not want to give them. So Jimmy took centre stage and told everyone that I was the woman he loved and that I had ditched him. He explained how he had almost begged me not to finish our relationship, but I had insisted, saying I needed time on my own and didn't want anything serious with anyone. Jimmy went onto say, "And now she walks through my mother's door with my brother, who also loves her because he has told me, and we are all supposed to be happy."

The mother just sat there. I was faced with a dilemma. There were two sons who both had strong opinions and Jimmy's girlfriend and a daughter and her husband. The tension was running high, and Jimmy's girlfriend was not happy. I was encouraged to stay, and when all the talking had been done the new bloke and I left.

Things were fine, or so I thought, until a few days later in the middle of the night Jimmy came pounding his fists on my flat door. He presented himself as that of a battered husband and his front teeth were missing. The girlfriend had attacked him and she couldn't stand the thought that I was back in Jimmy's life in any capacity. Jimmy was taken for immediate medical attention, and more attacks happened over the next year or so. Every time the attacks on Jimmy were made because I was back in his life. I felt terrible about this and several times attempted to end my relationship with the new man. Eventually after two years I called off my relationship after finding out some disturbing medical fact about the new boyfriend.

After this separation I was told by my brother that all the drug-related attacks on everyone I knew had been because the boyfriend had been getting drugs from the drug baron for free because he had been the one telling lies about my life, including insisting I was taking over the baron's drug patch. Because no member of my family knew my whereabouts and I never went for help from my family, his lies were believed by the drug baron and his gang.

***

During the same period I was out regular visiting the tramps in nearby towns and cities. When they finally accepted that I didn't work for the authorities I was made welcome to some of their packs. I learned some of their life stories and some were just heart wrenching. I understood why some thought it best to cut themselves off from the outside world and the societies that we live in.

***

After this relationship had ended I spent some time on my own and then eventually decided that I would have a relationship. Again disaster struck; this man had a mental condition that had not been diagnosed. He attacked me physically because he heard voices in his head. I made a decision that I would not have any more relationships; things were always too complicated and my life was already that. I had made some new friends along the way, and my attention had turned to a group set up for absent mothers. I found compassion and friendship within this group. It was a lifeline to my situation, and at long last I was able to allow some of the things that troubled me out into the open.

My health condition continued, waxing and waning all the time. Sometimes I felt ill for weeks at a time. I still was undergoing regular blood test to make sure nothing more sinister could be found, and if it had been then the doctor would have taken the appropriate action. The year was now 2006 and my health was taking another nose dive. I found that I could not eat, so I was sent to hospital to have a camera down my throat and to see a specialist about my stomach. This resulted in two conditions being diagnosed and referral to another department at my local hospital. After another 18 months of blood tests, I was diagnosed as having Hashimoto's disease. My immune system was attacking my healthy organs and my DNA was moving. This told the specialist that I was indeed ill. He advised that there was nothing that could be done about the DNA moving and when symptoms presented themselves they would be dealt with at the time. I was told the condition would only get worse as I got older. The specialist told me I had a lupus like condition also and would be referred to the department that dealt with that condition. It was explained further that the illnesses can be triggered by stress and that stress should be avoided at all cost. Now that was a joke! During this period, and by pure chance, I met in a casino Mrs. Anna Spacker. I was sat watching the roulette wheel when I was tapped on the shoulder, making me turn round to see who it was. I was shocked to find her stood there. We went for a drink and she was trying to make enquiries as to where I was now living and how I was in general. I gave her a load of lies. I was looking around all the time, thinking I was being set up by Fred, seeing that Anna was one of his old comrades. Fred didn't turn up and I sat with Anna until about 6.30am in the casino. I learned from her that while I had lived with Fred Roy had been part of a large group of criminals that were all operating under the control of Fred. She informed me also that Roy had not attended school since Fred had been released from prison at the beginning of 1995 and that a few days a week, Fred's criminals played out his crimes, she had looked after Roy to ensure he arrived home at the expected time so I wouldn't become alerted to the fact that he wasn't attending school. She told me Fred had attended several meetings at Roy's school and when he had been asked where I was he had said that I had been busy with the baby; every time he told them this. Anna told me that Fred had put a redirection order on all mail at my old Chesterfield address that's why I never got any mail. Fred had all mail redirected to the bed sit he was renting from Mr. Peacock; there he would determine what he was going to put through the letterbox of my home address. Fred knew that the post at that address didn't come till early afternoon and he used to go to his bed sit before seven in a morning because he knew that the post arrived at that address at or around that time. Everyone had known what Fred was doing with Roy, but no one dared tell him he was wrong for not letting him go to school.

Anna went on to say that Roy was made to sit and tell everyone present that he hated his mother. She said some people found this amusing; she said she didn't know what to make of his statements. Anna went on and on about things I had no idea about. I sat there listening in disbelief that educated people allowed this to happen to my child, or any child come to that, and did nothing and not even tell me until after the fact.

I asked Anna, "Why now?" She replied that it was because Fred had conned even more money out of her and her husband and by that time I had left my home address and they didn't know where I was. I didn't believe her explanations, and I knew she had been having a sexual relationship with him. Her husband had not got a clue who he was married to. I asked her if her husband had known that my child had not been attending school at the said time. She had replied, "No, he had been at work." At that stage I knew she was telling me the truth. I decided when I left that I would be contacting my solicitor because I wanted these incidents investigated.

Months later I was horrified when a report from Cas Cas arrived; it did indeed confirm all that Anna had reported to me. I wanted to make a complaint that I had not been informed of any absences that Roy had from school, but I was informed that the school could not be held responsible because Fred had presented himself as my son's legal guardian. What a load of bollocks! I now knew the world was an evil place; all these educated, responsible people could make incorrect decisions about my children's lives and not feel that they were in any way responsible for the outcome. It was perfectly clear that anything I had to say wasn't worth listening to. I swear I felt like I was going round the hat rack.

***

During this period Tina Chips was also back in my life, and she informed me that when she and her husband had given Fred money to cater their wedding they had allowed her only daughter to sign fraudulent cheques for Fred and she knew that Fred was giving her daughter money for this service every time she did this. When I asked her if it had achieved anything positive she didn't answer. I told her that her daughter would no doubt have been involved further than she would have ever realised, but she seemed to think she wouldn't have. She knew nothing about Fred—only the little she had experienced with the wedding. I now knew the daughter was on a road to destruction, and I knew Fred would have had some sort of input into that. The daughter turned to drugs and was arrested for numerous crimes including being found in possession of bullets. All Tina could say was "Where have I gone wrong?"

Chapter Thirty-One
The Dreams and the Italy Trip

For years I couldn't remember when I last had a good night's sleep. My dreams at times were very vivid and often repeated night after night. It didn't matter how I tried to address this sleep problem—nothing worked and I had to just accept this would be part of my life from now on. Nearly every day that I awoke from sleep I felt exhausted and every joint in my body ached.

One of the turning points in my life happened after a week of having a repeated dream. The month and year was June 2009. I could see in my dream someone who I presumed was a man. He was dressed in a white shroud and a gold light emanated around it. The figure had his hands open and out before him, and he said, "My name is Megatron. Do not be afraid. Everything will be all right." I could not see a face or anything above shoulder height; I just felt this beautiful warm feeling when he appeared. There was nothing suggestive to indicate that the figure was a man; it was more of an acceptance that it was a man and I had no reason to question anything different.

Megatron visited me night after night, and he always said the same thing. On his visits I felt upon waking that the visit had lasted hours somehow but when I recalled his visits I could only remember the same sentence, the same white shroud, and the gold light that shone all around the figure.

By this stage of my life I had met my husband Pedro in the year 2000 and we were married in 2006. Our lives were good, we both had good stable jobs and we had started travelling the world. Without realising, I was keeping my husband awake at night. He had never said anything to me until one day after the name Megatron was running around and around in my head I took the step to speak to my husband, Pedro, about the visitor in my dreams. For some reason the name would not move from my thoughts and it seemed like I had no choice but to say his name out loud. After speaking about my visitor and the only words he ever spoke to me in my dreams, Pedro told me that I had been saying the name out loud over and over again while I had been sleeping. I said I had no idea why I should be dreaming of a child's fictional figure, a Transformer. I couldn't recall watching anything in the past few weeks before the dreams had started or while they were taking place. I just knew it sounded crazy when I said it out loud but it had become worrying to me.

During the conversation and while Pedro was saying, "Next time he comes ask him for the winning lottery numbers," the house phone rang. It was a call from my stepson to his dad. During the course of that conversation Pedro had mentioned about the dream that I was having and he explained how he had said to get the winning lottery numbers. The stepson asked further questions. "What was said? What did the figure look like? Was anything else present in the dreams?" Pedro explained everything I had told him.

"It's not Megatron, Dad. It's Metatron," he said as a matter of fact.

Pedro questioned his son further, and once he came off the phone he explained what his son had said.

I immediately went on the Internet to look up the name "Metatron." If it was as the stepson had said; I needed to know more. There it was on the Internet:

Metatron

"The Throne Beside the Throne of God."

He is considered an Archangel and important at that. He is thought to have led the children out of Israel and also stopped Abraham from sacrificing his son Isaac. He helps us with our communication with God and helps bring God's presence to us. Even when we are being difficult he opens up our hearts so that we are more willing to receive God's guidance. He is also responsible for supervising the Akashic Records, which are a special archive where all our thoughts and deeds are recorded.

I read it out to Pedro.

"Well, why would this Archangel becoming to see me?" I asked.

The only thing I could come up with was all the trouble surrounding my children and what had happened to my mother. I instantly knew that was the reason, but I couldn't understand why he had been saying the same thing over and over again to me in his many visits. Was it because I was somehow going to have some sort of contact with my children? I doubted the thought as soon as it entered my head but felt there must be something meant by the repeated visits from Metatron. From then on I kept the visits in my mind, trying to dig deeper into my memory for anything that I had not remembered, but nothing came. I thought maybe he will come again and bring whatever message he wants me to know. But his visits stopped.

July of 2009 came round and Pedro and I were heading off for Italy. Neither of us had been and neither of us had ever taken such a long journey by coach. The holiday turned out to be a most memorable one and one we will take again. We stayed in a little village called Tignale, up in the mountains of Lake Garda. It was beautiful, the location couldn't get any better. The coach trip mainly consisted of much older people, and it was the first time either of us had holidayed with so many older people. It turned out to be one of the most memorable holidays we had taken.

Having arrived at the hotel, all guest were shown to tables that had name plates on, so people had to sit where they had been put. This was a first for both Pedro and me; we had always been used to sitting next to each other but on this holiday we were parted at the table seating arrangement but on the same table. At least that was a bonus.

After the evening meal everyone was sat talking and getting to know one another and conversation was flowing between everyone at all tables.

"He's going to ask you to go to the bar with him," a familiar voice came in my mind.

Before I could think anything a man in his fifties who sat next to me, asked, "Will you come to the bar with me to get a round of drinks in?" I could feel my heart starting to race and instantly thought "What the?"

"Yes," I found myself replying immediately.

Where did that come from? I sat rooted to the chair, the man oblivious to what had just happened and he was talking away, but not a word was going in as to what he said. I sat across the table from Pedro. I needed to get his attention; I needed to tell him what I had just heard. Was I going mad? My heart was racing even more.

"Well come on then. Let's go to the bar," the man said to me.

I rose from the chair, and Pedro looked in my direction. Now I had my chance to let him know I needed to speak to him. From the look on Pedro's face I knew he knew something was wrong. Pedro made his excuses and made his way to the bar area.

"Can I just have a word?" Pedro said to me as I was stood at the man's side at the bar.

Pedro and I moved out of earshot of everyone, and he asked what was wrong. I explained the events at the table.

"Don't worry," Pedro said "It will mean something."

"Don't worry," I said out loud. "I think I'm losing my mind, and you say don't worry?"

"You will be OK. If anything further happens let me know," Pedro said.

I felt ill momentarily. I recognised the voice and I knew it had been real. I returned to the bar and helped the man get the drinks in and back to the table. I was sitting in conversation again and had totally forgotten for a moment the earlier events of the voice when it returned.

"He's going to ask you to go to the Monastery tomorrow." The inner voice was as clear as a bell. My heart started beating faster and I knew enough was enough; I needed to get out of the situation I was in at the table. I was just about to get up and make some excuse when the man sat next to me said, "Would you like to come to the Monastery tomorrow with me and my wife? It's a beautiful place and I'm sure you and Pedro will enjoy it." I felt sick. Was it fear? or was I going to be ill? I hadn't a clue; I just knew I had heard that voice and again what had been said to me by the voice turned into reality.

"Yes," I replied.

Where did that come from? Again I felt that I wasn't in control of what I was saying.

Later that night I asked Pedro to reassure me I was not going insane. Pedro told me not to worry and that everything was going to be OK.

The following day went without incident. We all visited the monastery and what a beautiful and spiritual place it was. When everyone in the party had looked around the Monastery, we all gathered at the small café in the grounds for a cuppa. Everyone decided that one way or another we would make their way over or around the mountain to a little restaurant called Lily Anna's. A few people on the holiday had done the same trip several times before and knew the area quite well.

Pedro and I decided that we would take the path over the mountain and through the woods, following the man that I had sat next to the night before. On arrival everyone ordered something to eat and later made their way back to the hotel. The following morning a trip had been organised to Lake Garda and the lakeside. Everyone ate breakfast and boarded the coach. The journey should take about 20 minutes, they were told by the driver and instructions were being given about the time the coach would be leaving the lakeside. The sun was out and the temperature was hot. Pedro and I sat midway in the seating area on the coach. The coach set off to its intended destination.

"You're going to get a message from Liam. (He is my nephew.) He's made contact with your children," said the familiar voice in my head.

My heart started racing and in a second Pedro had noticed that something was wrong.

"What's up"? Pedro asked.

"I've just heard that voice again. It says...." I was interrupted by the text message sound on my mobile phone. I looked down at the screen and there was Liam's name flashing on the screen back at me.

"What? wh..?" Pedro went on to say.

I wanted to burst into tears and tried to hide my face so no one on the coach would notice. Pedro was insistent in his questioning.

"That voice told me I was going to hear from our Liam. He would tell me that he had made contact with my children, and now I've just received a message from him. I daren't open that message," I struggled to say.

"Open it, go on. We need to see," Pedro encouraged me.

I clicked on the message and there in front of me was the text message I had received from Liam.

It read, "I was going to wait till you returned from your holiday before I contacted you to say that I have made contact with your children on Face book. They are OK and we will speak more when you return home."

Tears just fell down my face, I sobbed as silently as I could. Pedro didn't know what to say. We both said nothing, having no idea what had just happened to me, but it was obvious that someone had a need to inform me of upcoming events.

The day passed and we were both dumbfounded with previous events, with me feeling really ill and anxious and Pedro sensing this. The holiday passed without further events, and upon returning home I had contact with Liam. The information that Liam had gleaned from the conversations on Face book was explained to me.

I made a decision to contact my youngest son via Face book messages. I had no idea how the contact would affect him and, to be truthful, myself. My youngest son returned my messages, repeatedly asking me the same question, "Why did you leave me? What went wrong between my dad and you? I have a right to know. Tell me."

I responded by telling my son he needed to ask his dad. I wanted to know if the scum bag would tell my son the truth once he had realised that contact had been made between us. I knew that he would know I would tell my youngest son the truth and I wondered how he was going to tell my youngest son. The message came back, "No you tell me." I really didn't want to spoil the surprise the scum bag would have received once he realised there was contact, but no matter how much the messaging went back and forth my youngest son reported that he wasn't with his dad and couldn't ask him. The youngest son became quiet forceful in his emails, and eventually I snapped.

"Go ask that murdering bastard why. Why he tried to murder my mother, your grandmother, and while you're at it go ask your brother as well. On top of all that you told lies about me and you took your own life into your own hands when you made false allegations about my treatment of you when you lived with me. You made your own choices and if something has gone wrong in your life I am not to blame."

The messaging continued along those lines until my youngest son just stopped email contact one day. I knew somehow that the youngest son would without a shadow of a doubt confront both his brother and his dad and I knew both would deny what I had told him. I was right. Late in the evening I had received an email from her youngest son while my PC had been turned off.

"You're a liar," it read. "I have asked them and you are lying! You will say anything and I don't want you to contact me again. Don't ever contact me, ever."

My heart just sunk and my temper was building inside me. I wanted so much to get hold of my youngest son and tell him to wake up. I sent an email back telling my youngest son that I was not lying; I was telling the truth. I couldn't help if he didn't like what he had read. But it was the truth. I could not make him believe me, but I couldn't expect him to react any differently and assured him that if he changed his mind he knew how to contact me. I felt really ill; it was a rollercoaster of emotions that ran from rage to pity for my youngest son. I felt so disappointed at the way my contact had gone with my youngest son, but I knew there had been no other way to address the reason for my departure from his dad's life and his oldest brother's life. I intended to start the way I meant to go on, and that was to say things the way that they had been and there was no way I was going to bevel under the pressure of these emotions. I would not give a false sense to my son, and he would have to either accept what I had said or sadly we would have to continue on these separate journeys throughout our lives. I had images of all three of them sat there and the youngest son being fed a load of lies about what I had informed him of, and they would be doing whatever they had to ensure that contact never took place again. There was no way they could allow the truth to come out to the youngest son. How does someone admit to such an evil crime? How does one justify such an act? How does one justify such deception? I sat and felt that was the end of the road in relation to a relationship to be had with my youngest son.

The next day I was trawling You Tube when I came across a song in a list of recommendations. There amid the list was a photo and I thought, "Hey up, that could be my oldest son," and I had an urge to click on the link. Right there staring back at me was a still photograph of someone who definitely had some characteristics of what I would imagine him to look like. The name on the post would be one that I could associate to him. I clicked on the link to play it. There on the screen was my eldest son singing a familiar song. I checked he had other videos on his site. I went through them listening, and one song in particular brought tears to my eyes. The pain was in my chest, with my heart jumping out of my rib cage. I felt that the whole world was closing in on me. Later in the day my temper got the better of me.

How dare he move on with his life? How dare he act as though he was just a normal person? Singing his head off for millions of people to view, and I knew the truth behind him. That was it. I couldn't help myself. I set about writing on his channel on You Tube and I told him exactly what I thought of him and how he had lied to his youngest brother. I was furious, even manic. How dare he present himself this way?

It was a Sunday morning; there was a knock at the door. Stood there were two WPCs. The constables had come to serve me with a document stating that I had harassed my youngest son, my eldest son, the eldest son's wife, and Fred. The document said I could not contact any of them including my eldest son's children. It was nothing that I hadn't expected, and I knew that I had rattled the nest, so to speak. I informed the officers that I had been expecting them and wasn't surprised. Then a PC asked, "What was it all about?" They had no idea. They had been asked to attend on behalf of Mansfield Police and hadn't a clue. That left way for me to speak about what had happened for the first time to an official person in all the years that had passed. It just flooded out; the women police officers just stood there. The main officer who had done all the speaking didn't seem concerned about what I had said and was showing this in her manner. This fuelled me more, and there was no way I was going to stop now that I had started to talk about it. Still the officers didn't seem interested. I could tell that they thought it was just me blowing off and advised that if the attempt on my mother's life was behind this then I should contact the police force in the area it had allegedly happened. I couldn't believe that I had just stood there and told the police about a serious crime and they didn't seem to care. That fuelled me even more. I told the officers, "Just serve me with what you have to then leave my home."

***

How dare the police not take on board what I had said? I was instantly catapulted back to the life I had lived with Fred. Again the police were protecting him and his actions. My mother didn't matter! The crime committed against this ill woman was no concern of theirs and they made that perfectly clear. I burst into tears.

***

Later that day, I picked up the phone and contacted South Yorkshire police to make the complaint of the attempted murder of my mother in 1995. The year was now 2009. In my opinion the police spoke as though they didn't believe what I was saying and informed me that I would need to call the police in the area that the alleged offence had taken place. Adamant that I would be heard I contacted Derby police, informing them that I did not want Chesterfield police to investigate my complaint of attempted murder against my mother. The police officer who took the call said he would make a note of what I had requested but didn't know if it would be possible for any other force to investigate my allegation. I stood my ground. In no way did I want the police officers who had instigated the initial meeting of my family and Fred involved in the investigation or the police force that had arrested both my brother and myself right back at the beginning of this journey of PAS. I made my feelings known that I would not be happy and that I wouldn't be heard. I informed the officer in Derby that the person who had tried to murder my mother was a registered police informer and the officers he worked for were based at Chesterfield police station and I did not want them involved at all. The officer said he would report what I had said to his inspector, but again he had no control of where the complaint would be dealt with. I was uneasy at the thought that now the two officers concerned would influence the course of this investigation.

Chapter Thirty-Two
The Murder Investigation

After being initially contacted over the telephone, the police from the Chesterfield area came to visit me at my home address. I had decided it would be better if I wrote the basis of my complaint on paper, especially with it being the police force I had initially not wanted to investigate my complaint. The officer's read what I had put in the statement and thanked me for doing it that way. They agreed it made it quicker and much easier for them to question me over the events of that night when Fred had tried to take my mother's life. They left saying they would get some information about the reason of death and they would be back in touch.

Over the next few days I was contacted by phone by various officers who had been assigned to the case. Then the call came that the two initial officers where coming back to talk to me.

When the officers attended again they informed me of the murder room for the investigation and how it had now been set up and they advised me that my mum's body may have to be exhumed for examination. I understood. They informed me that they were currently trying to locate both my mother's medical records and the call logs from that month and year before they could move forward with the investigation. Again I understood. The officers left.

A week or so later an officer who had been assigned to the enquiry called me to say that my mother's records had been destroyed because of the length of time involved and that the police were still trying to locate the 999 call that had been made in the month and year of my mother's death. A few days later the investigating officers attended at my home address to inform me that they were having difficulty tracing those records. Again they left saying they were doing everything they could to secure information before any arrest were to be made. They informed me that Rowan who had lived with me at the address where the attempt on my mother's life had taken place was proving hard to locate.

A week or so passed. Then I received a telephone call from one of the attending officers.

"We have had all three in custody. We questioned both your eldest son and Rowan who had lived with you at the time of the attempted murder. Both said they did not know what you were talking about. We then interviewed Fred and immediately he admitted that your mum had indeed accused him, but he said he did nothing. We have taken all the available evidence to the crown prosecution, who have informed us that there is not enough evidence to bring charges. However, my personal opinion is that I know from experience that Fred is guilty and I believe every word you have told us." The call ended with the officer saying that if ever in the future any information came to light they would reopen the case.

I had to accept that there was nothing further I could do, again because of the police and there treatment of me plus all other government departments. Fred had now got away with my mum's attempted murder. I just felt numb. If only I could have spoken before now.

Chapter Thirty-Three
St. Patrick's Day in Kenmare

There we were—Pedro, Lil, and me—in the jewel in the crown, Kenmare southern Ireland and it was St. Patrick's Day. We felt like we were at home in heaven. What a beautiful place, a place we visited often when work and circumstances allowed us to take a break. The day set off as usual with us all being in high spirits. We had all decided that we wouldn't frequent the local pub until after tea that day. Our intention was to go down to the town, have a look around the shops, and see how the day went before returning home to eat and then the pub for the evening. Our plans didn't turn out that way, though. As we entered the town we had to pass the local pub, one we went into every time we visited this town, and somehow we just found ourselves walking straight into the pub. We were greeted with the warm welcome we got every time we visited, and before we knew it we were all merry and it had got to the point that we had to eat. We were going to eat in the pub until Pedro reminded us we had put a roast in the oven on low before we had come out for the day, so we decided better got home and eat. As soon as we hit the home we were renting we entered the room, sat on the settee, and apparently Lil and I fell fast asleep. Pedro was left sitting on his own, listening to us two snoring our heads off. He sat watching TV, just waiting for us to come around before we ate. Laid asleep, something obviously disturbed me. I opened my eyes from sleep. I was focusing my eyes and there in front of me was an old man knelt and sat on his heels, wearing what looked like an old brown sack. He had a greyish-white short beard, and his hair was either short or thinning on top. He was sat in front of the open fire that wasn't lit, staring straight forward toward the room door. I lay there asking myself, "Who's he?" I lay on the settee for a moment trying to work out who he was, and then suddenly I shot up and Pedro was looking at me. The man just disappeared, vanished, gone, but where?

"Who was that man?" I asked Pedro.

"What man?" he replied.

"The man, who was just sat there in front of the fire?" I replied.

"There was no one there!" Pedro replied.

"Yes, there was. I saw him!" I insisted.

In the heat of all this Lil woke up.

"What's up? What's going off?" she asked.

Pedro was trying to convince me I was dreaming, but I was insistent a man had been knelt in front of the fire. By the time we had come around and eaten it was too late to go back to the pub. We promised each other we would not have a rerun of today's event's tomorrow. We had all wanted to spend St. Patrick's Day night in the pub and that had all gone by the wayside on this holiday. We ate our meal and sat watching the TV and talking into the small hours before we retired for bed. I explained to Lil what I had seen, and we came to the conclusion I must have been dreaming.

The following morning we decided again that we would spend the morning in the town before we would make off for one of the local attractions for the afternoon before our evening meal and then the local pub for the evening. It sounded good to all of us, so we set off for the town of Kenmare.

The town of Kenmare is so colourful; it is picturesque. Beautiful just doesn't seem to do the description justice. So there we are all over the moon that we were on holiday, browsing occasionally into the shops as we were passing.

"Let's try that pub at the top of the street," Pedro said.

"We don't want to get drunk again," I complained.

"We can go in and have a coffee. We don't have to drink. But all the times we have been here we have never been in that pub," Pedro said.

We all agreed; we hadn't been in that pub, so off we set to check it out. Walking up the high street I looked into a shop window and my heart just stopped beating. There staring straight back at me was the man's face that I had seen the night before in the living room of the home we had rented.

"That's him!" I shouted.

Pedro and Lil stopped and looked at me in surprise. I had shouted "That's him" so loudly, people were staring as they passed us by.

"Look—that's him! He was the man I saw last night in our room!" I said, pointing at the face on front of a book that stood in the shop window.

"Who is he?" I was asking.

"That's Padre Pio," Lil said.

"Who?" both Pedro and I asked.

"Padre Pio. He is a saint." Lil replied all matter of fact. Neither Pedro nor I had ever heard of him.

"Well, I'm telling you he is the man that was in the room last night." I said. "I'm going in and I'm having that book no matter what. He came to me and I want to know why. I won't take no for an answer!." I said, walking in through the shop door.

All the time we had visited this beautiful town I had never noticed this shop before, but Lil said she had once been to the shop on a previous visit to the town but the part of the shop where the book was displayed had been closed. I bought the book.

Even though we were on holiday I had a really strong urge to read the book, and I found it hard to resist temptation. When we got home later that afternoon I knew if I didn't put the book away I would have ended up reading it and then getting narked that I would have had to put the book down. I went upstairs and put the book away, telling myself when I got home that was on my immediate to-do list. We ate and then went to the pub. The book and Padre Pio were forgotten! The evening went well and we had a great time, Pedro and Lil doing the whiskey chasers that they always enjoyed when visiting Kenmare and me on the cider following the last drink of the night, a proper Irish coffee. You cannot get a proper Irish coffee anywhere other than Ireland! We set off back home feeling relaxed and we had all enjoyed the evening.

**

Later in the early hours of the morning I was woken by someone talking in my ear. Shocked, I opened my eyes, but no one was there. "I must have been dreaming," I thought and settled back to sleep. But clear as a bell I heard the following words, "You have won on the lottery! You need to go to town and check...hurry!." I sat up in bed and reached for the light switch. I turned on the light; there was no one other than Pedro lying fast asleep at the side of me. My heart was beating so hard I was in two minds to wake Pedro and tell him what had just happened but thought, "No I wouldn't be happy if a crazy person woke me and told me that they had just heard someone talking to them while they had been sleeping. And saying they had won on the lottery!" No, I wouldn't be happy so I turned off the light and went back to sleep. Hours passed by and at about 7 am I was woken again by the voice in my ear with the same message. That was it. I was getting up because there was no way I could sleep with the night's events.

I decided to go downstairs and make myself a cuppa. I'd leave Pedro asleep and tell him once he woke up what had been happening. I was in the kitchen when Lil walked in. She was shocked to find me there and was enquiring as to why I was up so early. It was nothing unusual for Lil to be up at this time but not me; that would have been a shock to anyone who knew me. I told Lil what had happened during the night, saying it seemed so real. She advised that I should go when the town opens up for business and check to see if I had won the lottery. There would be no harm, she assured me. Minutes later Pedro was down in the kitchen asking why everyone was up so early. I explained to him what had happened. There was no way I could go down town at that time so I would have to wait.

Later we set off downtown for the morning. Something inside me was saying that I was being stupid even thinking I could have won on lottery, but then there was another side of me saying I had. We got to the Internet café. I popped my money in the slot and went to access my emails because I was signed up for notifications by email if I was to ever win something on the lottery. There staring back at me was an email from the National Lottery saying they had some news about my ticket and advising I log into my account to see what I had won. My heart was beating so fast. Pedro and Lil stood outside the Internet café. I shot from the chair to the door.

"I have, I've won and I'm not kidding," I said in excitement. In a flash all three of us crowded around the computer as I attempted to access my account. What none of us had realised is that we could not access the site from southern Ireland. I would have to wait till I got home to find out what I had won. I think we were all disappointed that I couldn't find out, but there was nothing I could do until I got home.

The holiday went on and throughout the entire holiday I received the same message as I slept and every time I went to the Internet café to check my emails and every time there was an email from the national lottery telling me they had news about my ticket. It happened four times in all throughout that holiday, so you could imagine the frustration I was going through. Four different emails, four different tickets, knowing I had won something but not knowing what! Every day I would pick up that book of Padre Pio and I would get this peaceful feeling, a sense that it was him, whoever he was, but why he was making contact with me was still a mystery to me. I had to wait ten days to find out what I had won. I had contacted two members of my family back in Britain and told them what had happened and they too were inpatient for our return.

***

When we finally got home I had to wait a couple of hours for Pedro to get the PC from where we had taken it for safekeeping while we had been away. I immediately assessed my National Lottery account to find on each occasion I had won ten pounds.

Chapter Thirty-Four
The Dream

As we all know dreams can be a pleasant experience or nightmarish. Throughout all the years I was travelling on my life journey I think I had experienced most types of dreams; some had been terrifying, but they were only dreams.

In the year 2011 I started again to have dreams about Metatron. He used to speak to me about things playing roles at that part of my life. I always sensed I was at peace when I had these dreams/visions, call them what you must, and I felt refreshed in a silly way when I had woken. One night in 2011 Metatron had come calling and the message he gave me was as follows:

"When you awake in the morning call Ellen and Lil, and together all three of you go to Bluebell woods. Tell Ellen to take her camera!"

When I awoke the next morning this message was in my head and I was saying out loud, "Why?" Then I realised I had been dreaming and felt silly speaking out loud the way I had. The first hour or so I contemplated phoning both people, but in the back of my mind there was a voice saying "Don't be silly!." As I say I didn't really know what to do. I thought a while longer and decided these dreams/visions had always been for a purpose in the past and what did I have to lose by going to a local wood and doing what I'd been instructed to do? I rang Ellen and Lil to ask if either was busy that day and when both said they were free and wouldn't mind a walk in the woods, our morning plans were set. I asked Ellen if she would bring her camera and I explained I would tell all when the three of us were together. Lil and I arrived at Ellen's about 11 am. We all sat at the table and I told them both what Metatron had said to me. Neither of them laughed or ridiculed me because they both knew what had been happening to me in relation to theses dreams/visions. Without hesitation we set off for the local woods called Bluebell Woods.

We pulled up in the car alongside the wood in a small parking place close to the main path that ran through the woods. The area was very quiet, and looking at the path leading through the wood you could tell not many had walked it. Ellen took her camera from the boot of my car and we made our way to the path so we could walk through the woods. As we got to the path Ellen said, "So what am I supposed to do? Take pictures as we are walking if I see anything?"

Instantly I had the urge to say, "No!"

Ellen and Lil were looking at me to continue with some sort of instruction. I stood just looking back. I said nothing and because of this urge to speak out like I had just done, I thought, "Well, let's see if anything else happens." Nothing! We stood there about two or three minutes, and still nothing. All three of us did not really know what to do from this point on.

"Just take photos of the trees," I said.

I had no idea where that had come from either. So we set of walking, and Ellen was just aiming the camera at trees of all shapes and sizes, and she was clicking away, none of us really knowing why any of us were there. During the course of the next hour or so we were still in the woods I was telling them both some information I had been told years earlier by another friend of mine.

Apparently in years gone by there had been a factory in the general area, and it was owned by two men. Apparently one of the men and his wife worked because the children they had were at an age that they were nearly young adults. On returning home one evening they had discovered that their daughter was missing. This ensued a local search of the area, but still she wasn't found that night. The following morning her dead body had been discovered in Bluebell Woods. She had been stripped naked, her clothes lay out perfectly on the wood floor, and no one had ever been arrested for the murder. How true any of this was I had no idea. But it passed some time as we were walking. We didn't just stay to the main path for we would have walked the length of the woods in the direction the path through it led. We had decided early on that it would be best to get into the thicket of the woods where most people wouldn't generally walk. Ellen just clicked away, and Lil and I hugged trees; occasionally Ellen would have a hug too. We spent a good two and half hours going all way through this wood, and as far as we were concerned we had seen nothing out of the ordinary. We arrived back at the car, and we all agreed we had no idea why we were there. Ellen said she would upload all pictures onto her computer when she could find the time and she would email them to both Lil and me. We just accepted that we had to look at the pictures that had been taken on this outing.

Later in the early evening Ellen phoned me.

"Are you on the Internet now?" she asked.

"Yes why?" I replied.

"You're not going to believe what I have seen in the photos that were taken today. I will email you one in particular now," she said.

The email came through and I opened it. It was just a photo of a tree. The phone rang again. It was Ellen. "Have you got that email?" she asked.

"Yes, but it's just a tree!" I replied.

"Yes, I thought the same. Now look at the tree, but don't just look and think tree—look!" she instructed.

I looked again at the picture and there it jumped straight out at me.

"Oh my Lord!" I said. "I can't believe it! How on Earth didn't we see that?" I was shocked.

"I know! That's what I thought when I saw it. It sends shivers down your spine don't it?" Ellen asked.

There on the screen was a picture of a tree, the frosty wood floor, and nothing unusual about the scene until you looked at the trunk of the tree. There as plain as day was the figure of a young woman embodied in the tree trunk, naked, her arms straight up as though she was hanging by her hands. A miracle! Or was it coincidence? Lil was not at home when Ellen had called so she and Pedro flew across to the PC to look at the picture. Were all were struck dumb. Were we making ourselves see something we wanted to see? But how could we? We didn't go there with any instructions on what to photograph, and we had no idea what had been captured on the photos. We were there in the woods simply because I had dreamed about or been visited by Metatron and he had instructed me to go there with the said people. Without even talking about it we somehow just agreed that this was some sort of sign. But what sign? What did all this mean? I just sat back and thought, "Trees have spirits, and had the girl's spirit been entrapped within the tree? Was the tree showing anyone in the world who could see it that it was unhappy, and such a vile act against a human had been bestowed upon its branches?" And that's where my love of tree art began. Metatron had given me something to focus on— new hobby that didn't involve interacting with official bodies. It was something that nature herself could give to anyone who was prepared to open their eyes.

Over the course of the next couple of years I went on many tree hugging missions, and I found creatures and faces etched in the trunk of trees. Some were quite funny and I got pleasure from the pursuit, as did Ellen and Lil.

Word about the photograph of the girl in the wood travelled among our close circle of friends and family and everyone wanted to see. They all loved it. To my surprise when some people saw it they announced that they thought they had been going nuts for years because they too could see things in trees, nature, and buildings. That was it. Pictures from different locations around England started to appear in my in box. I was fascinated, as were everyone else who had the pleasure of looking at these photos.

I discovered that even on the street I lived we had tree art. I even pointed it out to people who reside here, and some had lived here all their lives and had never noticed faces or objects that could be seen in the trees on our road. I found the face of an owl in one tree and I named him Harold. I often hear people say "Hello" to him as they pass by and that puts a smile on my face.

***

I have travelled to a few countries in the world and no matter where I go I'm always looking for tree art. I even dragged Pedro up to Scotland on his only day off from work to take a photo of a tree my brother had passed and told me about. I couldn't see this one, but the description was fascinating. So along with Pedro, my brother Spring Heeled Jack, and sister-in-law we visited; here's the Wizard that we found. Without even thinking, a new group interest was born and it was something that we could all enjoy. Most important, this distraction had been born out of an old worn-out road that I had travelled for years.

Chapter Thirty-Five
Conclusion

I always thought the road would have no end, but the gods proved me wrong. They showed me that humans can either grow or stagnate. It was years of loneliness, torture, and being misunderstood and stigmatised. There is one thing I know for certain and that's if this can happen to me, it can happen to anyone.

Lightning Source UK Ltd.
Milton Keynes UK
UKOW03f0006040614

232810UK00001B/208/P